The last time you Sang to me

Crucial Lessons for an
Effective Worship Ministry

Silas Omoha

WESTBOW
PRESS®
A DIVISION OF THOMAS NELSON
& ZONDERVAN

Copyright © 2016 Silas Omoha.

All rights reserved. No part of this book may be used or reproduced by any means, graphic, electronic, or mechanical, including photocopying, recording, taping or by any information storage retrieval system without the written permission of the author except in the case of brief quotations embodied in critical articles and reviews.

WestBow Press books may be ordered through booksellers or by contacting:

WestBow Press
A Division of Thomas Nelson & Zondervan
1663 Liberty Drive
Bloomington, IN 47403
www.westbowpress.com
1 (866) 928-1240

Because of the dynamic nature of the Internet, any web addresses or links contained in this book may have changed since publication and may no longer be valid. The views expressed in this work are solely those of the author and do not necessarily reflect the views of the publisher, and the publisher hereby disclaims any responsibility for them.

Any people depicted in stock imagery provided by Thinkstock are models, and such images are being used for illustrative purposes only.
Certain stock imagery © Thinkstock.

Scripture quotes marked (NKJV) are taken from the New King James Version®. Copyright © 1982 by Thomas Nelson. Used by permission. All rights reserved.

Scripture quotations marked (NLT) are taken from the Holy Bible, New Living Translation, copyright © 1996, 2004, 2007 by Tyndale House Foundation. Used by permission of Tyndale House Publishers, Inc., Carol Stream, Illinois 60188. All rights reserved.

Scripture quotations marked (GNT) are from the Good News Translation in Today's English Version- Second Edition Copyright © 1992 by American Bible Society. Used by Permission.

Scripture taken from *The Message*. Copyright © 1993, 1994, 1995, 1996, 2000, 2001, 2002. Used by permission of NavPress Publishing Group.

The Living Bible copyright © 1971 by Tyndale House Foundation. Used by permission of Tyndale House Publishers Inc., Carol Stream, Illinois 60188. All rights reserved. The Living Bible, TLB, and the The Living Bible logo are registered trademarks of Tyndale House Publishers.

ISBN: 978-1-5127-6304-1 (sc)
ISBN: 978-1-5127-6303-4 (hc)
ISBN: 978-1-5127-6305-8 (e)

Library of Congress Control Number: 2016918484

Print information available on the last page.

WestBow Press rev. date: 1/6/2017

ENDORSEMENTS

The author of *'The Last Time You Sang to Me'* offers a compilation of his experiences as a worshipper in a way which reflects a relevant and current insight into worship, bearing in mind that worship at its heart, is an intimate activity with God. As you read along, you are certain to find the output of the book highly relatable and applicable, regardless of the setting, culture or expression of Christianity that you find yourself in. That in itself is reflective of the seasoned nature of the writer in the realm of worship, despite his relative youth. Regardless, he has communicated his nuanced outlook on choral matters with authority and conviction but combined with humility in his own inimitable fashion.

This literary piece is a thought-provoking piece insofar as you are a worshipper yourself –and reflects the heart of the author, who is a worshipper in the most all-encompassing sense of the word. I have experienced at close hand a handful of the plethora of experiences and empirical truths about choral matters and worship that he has shared in this book and on reflection, the alignment between what is in this book and how he has lived out his life has been near flawless. I commend this book to anyone who desires to gain a greater insight into the art of worship (individually or collectively) and who desires to gain a greater insight into further intimacy with God through the medium of praise and worship.

Ayo Afolabi
Youth Pastor, Jubilee House for All Nations, Essex.

'The Last Time You Sang to Me' illustrates the author's immense depth of knowledge and career in the music industry. His source of enlightenment bridges the gap amongst and between the leading musical genres of the 21st century. The book opens a pathway into the greatest techniques and strategies of the basis of worship. The reader not only encounters the struggles of a transitional transformation of corporate worship, but also encounters a personal worship with God.

Like never before, the curtains have been scaled back for the audience to catch a glimpse of what worship truly is. From the onslaught, the book takes the reader through a ride that elevates and surpasses the rhetorical understanding of music and its use in our generation.

Mike Aremu
International Gospel Jazz Musician & Saxophonist

Over the years I have come to understand that essentially, Worship is the key that unlocks the heart and door of heaven. When we truly understand and practice true worship we experience a genuine touch and encounter from God in His throne room.

There is a protocol to approaching God, but very few people know how to access Him through worship. Many people can sing but few really understand the dynamics of True Worship. In this book Silas has penned down from his own rich experience from being an effective Worship Leader, principles and practices to enable us begin to grasp those dynamics. I highly recommend this book and I trust as you start to understand and practice true worship you will begin to experience another dimension in your relationship with God.

Dr. Sola Fola-Alade
Lead Pastor of The Liberty Church London.

Worship is a fundamental pillar in our relationship with God: to walk closely with God the believer must understand the place and essence of worship. He must also understand that God is Almighty and by that it means He is God by Himself and He is God alone. He is self-sufficient, self-existent, self-reliant, self-sustaining, unchanging, all-powerful, all-encompassing, complete, and wanting nothing but deserving of our worship. When we worship, it is never for God's sake as our worship does not add to Him or make Him any better. There is nothing we do, say, give or hold back that can add, take away or make God any different or better than He is. Worship brings us into deeper union with God; in worship we behold Him in His awesomeness and majesty and this releases us to experience His realm of wonders. Through worship we are touched by God, our lives are transformed and we don't remain the same.

The need for all believers to understand worship, the kind of worship God deserves, the role worship plays in our union with God, congregational worship and leading worship can not be over emphasised; these are some of the valuable information saturated in 'The Last Time You Sang to Me'. This book is absolutely one of the very best instructional books on worship and worship leading that

I have read in recent times. Silas has put this work together out of his very rich experience that he acquired through many years of directing and leading worship across many churches, denominations and streams. He has served for many years as minister and worship director in our church, Victory Assembly Sheffield UK. He is a song writer, a passionate worship leader, and one of the very best at it. I see no one as more qualified to write this book. The lessons spread all through the eighth chapters of this book are worth finding. This book is a must read and I unreservedly recommend this great work to pastors and church leaders, worship directors and worship leaders, musicians and singers, anyone with passion for worship and anyone who is seeking to know more and give to God the best He deserves.

Dr. Musa Bako

Senior Pastor, Victory Assembly Sheffield & Author of The Love of Father God

I am amazed at the richness of this beautiful curious work on worship. It could easily be referred to as *"The Bible of Worship"*. Reading through it, you are left in no doubt what worship truly is, how to do worship and the different dimensions of worship that there is. In all, the most outstanding part of the book for me is how it well summed up the expectation and the longing of God to a genuine worship.

In the present dilemma of who worship is supposed to satisfy - God or the worshipper, the classic highlight of the worship pitfalls brings it home that we have got no excuse to avoid whatever may want to rob or disqualify us of the pre-occupation and lifestyle of worship. Worship leaders, choirs, musicians/instrumentalists and the generic worshipper will find the book extremely useful to align them and to satisfy the worship spec that command God's attention. All I could say to myself after reading the book is, 'why worship if it is not worship?'

I would like to salute the openness and deliberateness in the approach of this author, to not just bring knowledge, wisdom and understanding to worship, but also he has used the book to bring purpose and essence to worship and I would like to commend this book to all lovers of God. Remember, why worship if it is not worship?

Tunde Balogun
Senior Pastor, Kingsborough Family Church London

For as long as I've known Silas, he consistently demonstrates a profound and in-depth understanding of scriptures and the dynamics of worship. I've come to appreciate there is a unique grace on his life, for tapping into that special place when hearts and songs are lifted in Worship to the Most High. I am thoroughly excited about his book; 'The Last Time You Sang to Me'. The author's deep insights on worship and choral matters is likely to bless you, as it has blessed me. This fascinating exposition is gripping and refreshing; especially if you find worship and contemporary Christian discourse intriguing. The book raises salient food for thought and offers proven and tested solutions to some of the issues you may have come across in modern Church Culture.

Charles Deji Juba
Singer & Songwriter, Fourkornerz

It is interesting indeed, how we could be ministers of music in Churches, tantalizing people with our gifting and musical dexterity, yet God may not have heard our voices in a while. And for several of us, that 'while' could be a very long one…So, if you want to know what separates your voice from the myriad of voices; if you want to know how to be heard from Heaven without glitches or break in transmission; how to be sanctified; if you want to know how to fulfil purpose as a music minister, this book, *The Last Time You Sang To Me*, by my amiable, principled and humble brother, Silas Omoha, is highly recommended. You wouldn't have read through half of its pages before you know that the solutions he proffers are scripture based; time tested, and trusted, and also from a deeply rich experience that spans over decades and continents.

Kenny K'ore

Singer & Song Writer

As the head of International Ministries at Yoido Full Gospel Church the one language that has woven our congregation of over 40 nations into one has been worship. Worship has a transcendent quality that makes it one of the most powerful tools for an ever-globalizing society. Silas Omoha's thorough undertaking of Worship Ministry is for both novice and veteran. *The Last Time You Sang To Me* proves to be both axiomatic and pragmatic. Wisdom is reaped from these pages.

Rev. Yoon Lee

Head of International Ministries, Yoido Full Gospel Church
(Seoul, Korea)

Being in the worship ministry brings with it, some pretty big challenges. The act of coordinating the choir, the musicians, getting the right songs to minister in services, dealing with diverging opinions in a worship team and maintaining a consistent connection and right standing with God are some of the roles of a worship minister. I have seen the author excel in all of these areas as he continues to become less in order that Christ might be more in his life.

This book captures all of these and throws insight to the inner workings of corporate worship. After all is said and done, God is seeking true worshippers who will worship Him in Spirit and truth. Therefore, it is in our interest to make it a priority to become such worshippers.

"The Last Time You Sang to Me" elucidates the essentials of the worship ministry in very clear and relatable terms. This stimulating and thought provoking book is guaranteed to inspire the reader unequivocally. I will recommend this book to everyone and not just for those in the worship ministry.

Abimbola Komolafe
Senior Pastor RCCG Jubilee Church Manchester.

"The Last Time You Sang To Me" offers refreshing insight into the realm of praise and worship in the evolving context of present day Christianity. Boasting impressive knowledge of the practical and spiritual responsibilities of a choir, the author's deeply personal narrative offers an intriguing perspective on the emerging issues

surrounding successful worship ministry. Rightly identifying God as the critical recipient of praise, worship and thanksgiving, the book extensively explores the varied nature of corporate and personal worship while simultaneously delving into scriptures to illustrate these distinctions. The clear analysis of presented challenges facing worship leaders and choral ensembles, coupled with practical techniques, best practices and solutions, make this book a particularly useful resource.

Niyi Ojuolape

Lead Pastor, Desire of Nations—Manhattan, New York

Isn't it true that a man cannot give what he does not have? Some write out of research, some write out of experience, some write out of academic studies, some write out of knowledge, some write out of passion…etcetera. Silas epitomizes worship, lives worship and tries to model worship. No wonder this book is revelatory, inspiring, passionate, Holy Spirit birthed and certainly life changing. It is a resource tool for the budding worshiper, for choral groups and Churches. It's a practical tool for all categories of believers. It's a needed message for the body of Christ at this hour.

Thank you Silas for making yourself available to be used of God to put this compendium together. Highly recommended and needed. **"The Last Time You Sang To Me"** is an excellent material from an excellent man of God.

Dr. David Sola Oludoyi

Regional Pastor: RCCG Europe Mainland Region 3 & Senior Pastor, RCCG Royal Connections London.

ACKNOWLEDGEMENT

When the idea of writing a book was first suggested to me, a few people played vital parts in the creative process. As I compiled the list, I found it fascinating that a number of Tolus had been pivotal at the start and in the end. First, Tolu Olajide. Thank you for 'pestering' over the need to complete the book. To Tolu Akinyemi, your constructive feedback was the game changer. I thank you for helping with the ideas for the title of the book, and for the recommendations you made. To Tolu Abiona, as always thank you for the useful tips you share, especially when we had to choose the right publishing firm to go with. To Toluwani Daramola; thank you for expediting the book completion process. Lastly, To Toluwani Oyewale, thank you for the brainstorming sessions.

I owe gratitude to: Ayo Afolabi, Arinola Nnatuanya, John and Odun Okeme, Seun Akindele, Sam Aderounmu, Ayo Thompson, Bayode Akanbi, Demi Gbenle, Dami Gbenle, Olumide Omotayo, Shola Adegbite, Kemi and Seye Samuel-Onalaja, Prince Ekpemandu, Kemi Ogunmoye, Leke and Titi Adeboye and Omotoye Makinde for your constructive feedbacks and contributions throughout the creative process of the project. I specially thank Charles Deji Juba and Damola Ladipo for your painstaking effort in working out a good cover design, and in the proofreading of the manuscript respectively. I also thank Martyn Smith for helping with additional editing of this work.

I must offer grateful thanks, to Pastors Bimbo and Folu Komolafe. The original idea of this work was inspired under your tutelage and counsel. I value the experience of being a part of God's assignment for you both in Manchester; and for your unparalleled support, which has remained unflinching.

I am also indebted to Pastors Musa and Eunice Bako. I thank you for the platform to serve as Worship Director for High Call and Victory Assembly, Sheffield. Your trust, hand of fellowship, teachings, counsels and the exposures you permitted has made this project possible.

I thank Pastor Agu Irukwu and the RCCG UK Executive Council for providing the platforms that has paved way for me to grow in the faith. Your simplicity and spirit of excellence has shaped many of us towards the mark of the high calling.

To all of Ancient Landmark, Choral Matters, High Call, Riversongz, Special Treasure, and Spirit & Life Choir. I thank you for your hand of fellowship and the shared experiences that led to the conception and completion of this book.

To my dear sister, Iyefu; thank you for encouraging me and walking me through the decision to go with Westbow Press. To my brother, Aboje— you are refreshingly blunt, and that has helped.

To Reggie Adams, Rick VanDeventer and the Westbow Press Team, thank you for your professional support.

To Pastors Sola and Tumise Ewedemi, your encouragement and support has been inspiring and pivotal to the emergence of this book; and for everything else, I'm thankful and grateful.

I thank Pastors Wale and Dupe Afolabi, for the hand of fellowship extended to me time and again, for the platforms to serve under your esteemed watch and for the relentless support you have given me over the years.

I thank Pastors Sola and Grace David Oludoyi for being a pillar of wisdom and encouragement. I appreciate the many ways you have expressed pastoral care. I honour and celebrate you both, especially for accommodating me in my first days in the city of London.

I'm indebted to my biological parents, Lexy and Asabe Omoha for many reasons. First, the foundation of my Christian faith was allowed to blossom in a conducive atmosphere and in a peaceful, loveable and friendly home. Second, your investments and faith in me has made me who I am today, by the grace of God.

I specially thank my spiritual parents, Pastors Enoch and Folu Adeboye for their visionary and exemplary leadership and their commitment to the Lord which has profited me in several ways.

In every way the first, and in no way the least; I owe gratitude to God; To His Son, Jesus; the Captain of my Salvation and the Owner of my heart; To the Holy Spirit; the Spirit of Truth, the Secret of my Strength, my irreplaceable One True Companion and the Eternal Voice of Reason.

CONTENTS

- Foreword xvii
- Preface xx
- Chapter 1—*The Role and Job Description of a Choir (Chorister)* 1
- Chapter 2—*The Dynamics of 'Corporate' Worship* 15
- Chapter 3—*The Element of Excellence in Corporate Worship* 35
- Chapter 4—*The Average Challenges of a Choir* 49
- Chapter 5—*The Pitfalls in Music Ministry* 68
- Chapter 6—*The Secret Character of the Worship Leader* 89
- Chapter 7—*Singing and Remaining as One* 103
- Chapter 8—*After All Is Said and Done* 118
- Glossary 127
- Bibliography 130

FOREWORD

Worship—an integral part of service to God and man, has a force that draws men to God, when properly done in the spirit, and not in flesh. The author of this book makes us realize that God as an invisible entity does not just accept anything offered to Him, except it is done in an attitude of worship- in spirit and in truth. Hence he makes it clear that Choirs are not designed to entertain or while away the time before the "Main" event or service. Rather, they are to offer profound renditions that will connect men to their Maker. He emphasizes the role of Choristers and Musicians as stewards and vessels designed to minister to the Lord by singing praises to Him, minister to the saints through worship, linking their spirit man to their Creator and even prophesying to their situations and of course, wet the appetite of the congregation in receiving the Word of life. Thus, making the Pastor's work easy.

Also in this book, the author highlights what can make Corporate-Worship enjoyable: Language: no matter how scripture-based a song is or highly anointed the songs are, if the language is not understood by the worshippers, their spirit will not be connected to God. He, therefore suggests an interpretation to a universally understood language, i.e. English, so that no one is denied the joy of the presence of God during worship. Visual Aids: Visual aids help to make a difference, especially for the targeted audience. They connect better when they know the wordings of the songs presented, and adaptability to your environment when importing a song from a different cultural background. e.g. pronunciation of some words. Also, our dressing and presentation should be a reflection of Christ.

Moreover, in this book, you will discover "Excellence" should be a touch of whatever you do for God particularly in your renditions. It touches down on your enunciation and articulation and the likes. Excellence propels you to pay attention to details and seek to promote the very good standard and good value to what you do for God. Additionally, because God is excellent, his name is excellent, and since he is excellent in power, therefore offer your services to Him in an excellent manner. One other thing you will also come across in this book is the fact that resources should be made available for effective songs ministration because the author said and I quote *"Without the instruments that help unify our singing, our songs would be chaotic and very displeasing to listeners"*. Of course, he places a premium on the issue of discipline and dedication on the part of the choir members to produce a satisfactory balance.

Going further, the writer points out that a life of prayer, study of the Word and a life of holiness serve as the foundation and secret of effectiveness and productivity in the worship ministry. One of the statements that struck me most in this book; and I believe will also challenge you whether you are in the singing ministry or not, is the issue of being a SIGNPOST. You cannot afford to show others the way to Heaven while you are locked out because of failure to please the one who saved you and set you apart for His use.

As a person who started in the ministry as a member of the Choir in the church, I strongly and sincerely recommend this book to Pastors, Worship leaders, Choir members and all who care to render an acceptable worship and service to God. I believe this piece will not only transform your life but enable you to birth transformation in the lives of people around you–particularly those in the singing ministry. May the Lord enrich your life as you go through the pages of this book.

Pastor Margaret Daramola.
Wife of the *Assistant General Overseer, The Redeemed Christian Church of God.*

PREFACE

'...I've had all I can take of your noisy ego-music.
    When was the **last time you sang to me**?
Do you know what I want?
    I want justice—oceans of it.
I want fairness—rivers of it.
    That's what I want. That's all I want.'
—Amos 5: 23-24 (*The Message*)

In the Summer of 2003 I had become part of a fairly new church plant in the city of Manchester as an International Student from Nigeria. Prior to that, I had just moved from London after my A-level examination, and as a part of my extracurricular activity, I reluctantly agreed to join the choir. The truth is, if it had been up to me alone, I probably might have preferred to remain an usher as I once was, or in a department less prominent than the Worship Team, but word had already spread to the pastorate about the arrival of a 'fresh young choir leader' and I was appointed before I could even say Jack Robinson. As I was much younger at the time, I lacked maturity— I had a lot of passion and zeal but lacked tact, wisdom and people skill. This became decidedly apparent at my first rehearsal. It appears, I must have caused a row at my first rehearsal, and information had quickly reached the Pastor who was returning to Manchester from a Ministers' Conference in Bognor Regis. When he was told that the choir practice had been largely disrupted by this new fellow, he picked his phone and rang me to get a balanced perspective of what might have taken place in his absence.

As it stands, I no longer recall the exact details of the conversation. However, I do remember, that I had vented my displeasure over the situation I had met on ground. I didn't mince my words. The choir as I saw it was a joke and a corrective measure had to be put in place. Fortunately for me, he seemed very calm about what I had to say, and simply advised me to put it in writing. That incident led to the first journal of the chronicles of my worship experience. Today, I admit that I still have a lot to learn and I thank God also, that over the years, I have found better ways to express my views on the many matters we deal with as a choir and as a Church. These journals and my many questions of 'why', 'when' and 'how' would leave me with a million nights of meditations and a search for the answers to my numerous questions.

Eventually, I found the answer to one of my many questions about the Worship Ministry in Amos 5: 23-25. In this scripture, we find that songs rendered to a God who is not visibly seen or audibly heard can be a challenge in some instances. The invisibility of God, although He is ever-present automatically produces two perspectives to the outcome of our rendition. First, you have our perspective here on earth, and second, we observe that God may equally take a similar or different perspective to our worship experience. Cain offered God burnt sacrifices only to discover that it wasn't good enough as far as God was concerned. Again, from this scripture, if I were asked, *'when was the last time you sang to me?'* I would imagine at the least, three inferences and dimensions to what is being said or asked:

(i) I haven't heard your voice in a long while
(ii) I do not remember the last time you sang to Me
(iii) When was the last time you **really** sang to Me?

If such a question is posed to any person in a dialogue between God and the individual, this should naturally inspire a moment of reflection. This book offers a reflection of some of the dynamics of the worship ministry from five angles. Firstly, the purpose and reasons for establishing a worship ministry are examined. Secondly, it points out the difference between an individual's personal time of worship from one that involves others. Thirdly, an exposition for excellence in the worship ministry is carried out for the benefit of those who view it from opposing angles. Fourthly, the book reviews the challenges and the pitfalls associated with the worship ministry, and finally, a reminder of what the ultimate goal of every Christian should be is presented.

Anecdotes from my personal experience and personal standpoint are used at the start of each chapter. This is then followed by an exposition of the various subjects discussed in the book. Attempts have been made to support each line of thought with relevant portions of the Bible, and from some leading commentators in the fields of theology and the worship ministry. Jargons and words which possibly lack a global or wide understanding are *italicised* and explained in the glossary. Furthermore, while the definition of what a choir and worship team may differ to some, in the context of this book, they mean the same thing and are used interchangeably.

Finally, an exhaustive list of the references used in the footnotes can be found in the bibliography.

As you read on, I hope you find the contents beneficial, edifying and helpful in your worship experience and ultimately in your Christian walk with God.

Enjoy your read!
Silas Omoha

CHAPTER 1
The Role and Job Description of a Choir (Chorister)

This people have I formed for myself; they shall declare my praise.
—Isaiah 43: 21

As a millennial born and raised in middle-belt Nigeria, I have a vivid recollection of a childhood characterised by Sunday churchgoing and singing at morning mass. Heightened by my parents' decision to send me off to a Catholic boarding secondary school, I found myself sentenced to the singing of the *'Nicene Creed', 'the Kyrie', 'the Penitential Acts'*, and whichever recitation was sung in the *Liturgy*. If memory serves me correctly, I also remember one of my friends often remarked that I tended to sing out of tune, and he did so with delightful disdain. He did this at nearly every mass where we sat next to each other. To be frank, I cared very little of what his opinion of my singing was. Young as I was, one fact was clear at the very start. The singing was personal and between God and me. Moreover, as far as I was concerned, God was the focal point of the exercise. Now the prevailing point of this story is that today I am rather able to sing in tune and in key. Ironically, it so happens that my good friend eventually became one of those who looked up to me, as far as singing was concerned.

As months turned into years, I made the best and most significant decision in life when I accepted Jesus into my life as personal Lord and Saviour. That divine encounter led to a journey of many attempts to be totally devoted to His service. Over the years I have come to realise that many like me joined the choir by providence and with little knowledge of both the practical and theoretical rudiments of music; and with no particular conviction of what exactly the job of a chorister from God's perspective entails. This affirms what has been rightly said. 'When purpose is unknown, abuse is inevitable'.[1]

In many choirs today, there are people like me who at the start of their membership, may not particularly know what the function of a choir and the duty of a chorister is. In some instances, this leads to a number of challenges, which in turn produces some of the issues visible in many choirs today. On this premise, a discussion on choral matters— or the worship ministry, if you prefer— should begin with an outline and overview of what a choir or chorister's job entails. Choirs are not designed to entertain or while away the time before the 'main' event.[2] Those who hold such views whether they do so from what they say typically at a gathering of Christians or through their actions or inactions are misinformed or misguided. If this is the case, what then are the role and function of the choir, as a corporate entity?

First, we find the answer in 1 Chronicles 25, where David formally sets up a Choir with a defined job description.

---

[1] Myles Munroe, *Understanding the Purpose and Power of a Woman*, (New Kensington: Whitaker House, 2001), 1—2.
[2] Enoch A. Adeboye, *"The Role of the Choir"*, (lecture presented at the annual general meeting of ordained ministers of The Redeemed Christian Church of God UK, London, November 18 2004).

> *King David and the leaders of the Levites chose the following Levite clans to lead the worship services: Asaph, Heman, and Jeduthun. They were to proclaim God's messages, accompanied by the music of harps and cymbals. This is the list of persons chosen to lead the worship, with the type of service that each group performed.*
> —1 Chronicles 25:1 (GNT)

This job description includes the following:

- ✓ To prophesy with music (1 Chronicles 25: 1).
- ✓ To give thanks and praises to God (1 Chronicles 25: 3).[3]

This is the reason why choirs are allocated slots at church services to minister to God's people through what is now termed a special song, special number, ministry rendition, or song ministrations. It further justifies the choir's role in leading the worship, thanksgiving and praises to God. Furthermore, prophecy within this context hint at a message for God's people through the songs delivered. I remember a number of times when people would walk up to me or another member of the choir after a worship service to thank us for singing a particular song that resonated with what they were passing through at that point in time. There were also occasions where we would rehearse a particular song. Then for one reason or the other, we get forced to postpone the delivery date, only to find out that the delay was worth it in the end. A choir positioned at the heart of God's purpose will prophesy through music and will invariably help people

---

[3] Outline based on the King James Version Translation of 1 Chronicles 25: 1, 3.

express the relevant emotion that connects them to God through the choice of songs that have been prayerfully selected and are Spirit led.

Second, as a singular unit, choristers and musicians are stewards, and vessels designed and appointed with purposes and primary roles: These include the following:

- to minister to the Lord *(2 Chronicles 13: 10, Ephesians 6: 6—7)*.
- to minister to (others) God's saints *(Hebrews 6: 10)*.
- to aid the Pastor *(2 Kings 3: 15)*.
- to serve the Lord as a co-worker *(Exodus 8: 1, 1 Corinthians 3: 9, and 2 Corinthians 6: 1)*.
- to be filled with the Holy Spirit and to edify with psalms, hymns and spiritual songs *(Ephesians 5:18—19)*.[4]

Thus, a choir is set up with two principal functions: (i) to proclaim God's message through music and (ii) to worship God. In effect, this means that there are two primary elements involved: God and man. First, it is God who inspires and instructs on what message is to be delivered. Second, God is the due recipient and receiver of thanksgiving and praises. God's glory is not to be shared with others[5]. On the other hand, songs which convey messages from God are to be delivered to the saints. One example of a song that is targeted at the saint is a song by Shirley Caesar titled *'You're Next in Line for a*

---

[4] Adeboye, *"The Role of the Choir"*.
[5] See *Isaiah 42: 8 and Revelations 4: 11*.

Miracle'.[6] God is not in need of a miracle. He is the miracle worker and miracle giver. Hence, the song is directed at man, and not at God.

Then there are other songs with a mix of both elements: a part of the song focuses on the individual, and the other part focuses on God. For instance, lyrics from the song, *'Everlasting God'*— *'Strength will rise as we wait upon the Lord, we will wait upon the Lord'* can be helpful in the time of physical, emotional or spiritual weakness. In this song, Brenton Brown introduces a switch at the chorus, where God becomes the focal point—

> *'<u>You</u> are the Everlasting God,*
> *<u>You</u> do not faint,*
> *<u>You</u> won't grow weary.*
> *<u>You</u> are the Defender of the weak,*
> *<u>You</u> comfort those in need*
> *<u>You</u> lift <u>us</u> up with wings like eagles.'*[7]

By that accounting, we could bear these factors in mind, in the song selection process; observing what is needed at each point in time. We fix our gaze on God in our choice of songs and at the same time, we remain sensitive to the needs of the congregation.

Implicitly, this means that as a choir—and if we individualise it, as a chorister —you are expected to have a relationship with God,

---

[6] Shirley Caesar, *You're Next in Line for A Miracle*, Word Entertainment LLC, 1997, CD.
[7] Brenton Brown and Ken Riley, *Everlasting God*, Integrity Music, 2006, CD.

and with the people of God. For this reason, giving of thanks and the praise and worship is to God, and not to the congregation. The receiver and recipient of that aspect in a church service is God. For example, if I sang *'Lord You Are Good and Your Mercy Endures Forever'*[8] last Sunday to God, then it should not be a problem to repeat the song the following Sunday, if in my heart there is a need to reaffirm that God and a need to re-emphasise his never-ending mercy.

The point here is, the praise worship should not aim to impress people, it should be a means of expression to God based on relationship, for what he has done, and for who He is. If he has healed you, or delivered you from a ghastly accident, or protected you, or done something specific to you as an individual, or perhaps showed you mercy, or done all these together, then your worship should reflect an expression of thanksgiving for what God has done. What this does is that it keeps God as the recipient of the worship.

However, this does not excuse the significance of being accountable to fellow worshippers. I shall explain what I mean with a hypothetical example. Imagine I have a friend who is proficient in English and French. Also imagine that, this hypothetical friend who is born to Ivorian Diplomats and has lived in Canada, Cote D'Ivoire, England, Nigeria and France. While in England, he learns a song with a popular lead on the gospel music charts. He notices that whenever this song is played on the radio or sung at a Christian gathering in

---

[8] Psalm 100: 5

England, everyone around him takes a reverential position in the place of worship. The words of the song in English are: *'Our God Is Greater, Our God Is Stronger, Lord You Are Higher Than Any Other'*.

My hypothetical friend is then invited to lead worship at a Christian Festival in France. With his proficiency in French and English, he selects some French songs that a good majority of the congregation happen to know. However, as he sings along, he is tempted to sing 'Our God Is Greater'. He tries to translate it into French, but he doesn't enjoy his attempted translation. So he switches back to English and sings the song in the original version. Now even though God understands every language and may have no problem receiving my friend's worship in English. Nevertheless, there are other people involved in the worship who do not understand what he is singing. As a result, the dynamics of the worship experience changes. At that point, as a collective corporate body, there has to be a reasonable consensus in how God is worshipped at the festival. By consensus, some considerations become vital. This will naturally include: language, time and duration of the worship, and the structure and order of how the worship is to be conducted[9]. In the next chapter, this is discussed in detail.

Third, the choir functions in the ministry of helps.[10] A purpose driven choir aids the ministry of the pastor, teacher or prophet.

---

[9] See *1 Corinthians 14: 40*.
[10] Kenneth E. Hagin, *Understanding the Anointing*, (Tulsa: Faith Library Publications, 1983), 76

Elisha was a beneficiary of the ministry of a minstrel in 2 Kings 3: 15. In order for Elisha to be effective in his own office, he required the assistance of a musician who was filled with the Spirit of God to bring down the Holy Spirit.[11] Israel's first king, Saul was also a recipient of the effective music ministry of David. In 1 Samuel 16: 15—23, we notice that Saul was refreshed and became well whenever David played the harp.[12]

I recount an experience a preacher once shared about his trip to Haiti a few years ago. As I recall, the Man of God was exhausted by the enormous amount of trips he had embarked upon back-to-back, with Haiti being the last lap of his tour for the week. Yet, in spite of his physical and mental exhaustion, he had one more preaching engagement for the evening and as a result hoped that God would strengthen him for the final lap. In answer to his prayers, the moment his Saxophonist who preceded him in the program of the day began to play; he felt re-energised and refreshed physically and supernaturally. This is one example among many others. Some preachers attest to the fact that the worship can either help the flow or disrupt their flow when things are either done right or done inappropriately.

Fourth, choristers and musicians serve God as co-partners and as a part of God's body.

---

[11] Adeboye, *"The Role of the Choir."*
[12] *Ibid.*

'For we are both God's workers. And you are God's field. You are God's building.[13] In other translations, those of us who fall into this category are described as co-partners with God. Most churches tend to use varying terms to describe their volunteers. However, whether workers, volunteers, co-labourers, co-partners, or staff of the Church organisation, here we refer to the subject of human resources. In consequence, an understanding of these concepts should change the paradigm and attitude of members of the worship team who serve the Lord globally. A labourer or worker is expected to do a job—WORK! The reason why this subject is a fundamental starting point for the worship ministry is because, so many people join the choir with different expectations. You find people who presuppose that singing is a simple exercise everybody should be able to perform, and thus, everyone who wishes to join the choir should be given the chance and opportunity to do so, even when some are unwilling to 'labour'. As a co-worker with Christ, things have to be put in the right perspective.

In the first place, God Himself is a worker. We are invited to work along with Him. Although He works within divine invisibility, visibility, mortality and immortality, we work alongside him visibly.[14] Our inability to see God in the present does not reduce the extent of God's involvement as a worker in the body of Christ. What this means is that, a chorister or musician should see themselves as a

---

[13] 1 Corinthians 3: 9 (NLT)
[14] See *Colossians 1: 16 and 1 Timothy 1: 17.*

junior partner[15] with a hardworking God. If the choir rehearsal starts at 5pm, a good partner should understand that, my senior partner is holy, pure, just, righteous, and would be there at 5pm. Punctuality and indiscipline in the choir is only an issue where those who claim to work for and with God lack understanding of Whom, they are working for and working with.

In addition, you may have come across some members of the worship team who, on some occasions portray an attitude of nonchalance to their service in the Church. To be all the more precise, it is inconsistent to be punctual to work at 9am in the morning, punctual when you have an interview, or an examination, or perhaps a business appointment, and yet unpunctual to rehearsals and church meetings. Most of the times, the reason for this inconsistency is simple. The interviewer, manager or supervisor can be seen with the physical eyes, whereas God, although real, mainly operates as an invisible deity where He is not seen physically in the present age. Hence, subconsciously nonchalance and excuses are often self-justified.

In the second place, as a fellow worker, it should be understood that the Father works, Jesus works, and the Holy Spirit works.[16] Jesus affirms this position when he told the Jewish authorities in John 5: 17, *'my father is always working, and so am I.'*[17] As for the Holy Spirit, we can also affirm that he works in every believer. He is the Actor who

---

[15] David Y. Cho, *The Holy Spirit, My Senior Partner*, (Lake Mary: Charisma Media, 1989), 7—12
[16] See *Ephesians 3: 20*
[17] *John 5:17, NLT*

helps our infirmities whenever we become limited by human factors. Therefore, if the Father, Son, and Holy Spirit are busy engaged in the work of the ministry, then what is my excuse and what could be yours?

The chorister also functions as a worker in God's vineyard with an additional understanding in view. Beside the fact that God himself works, it is crucial also to note that the devil also works. God's word affirms this in John 3: 8 where it states that the Son of Man was made manifest for a specific reason; to destroy the **works** of the devil. This means that Jesus came to destroy the devil's labour, and as a co-worker together with Christ, our role is to be battle axes and vessels God can use to establish his purposes and plans all over the world.

From this perspective, a chorister should recognise their role and purpose as prophets (God's messengers) who serve in the music ministry. They invariably function as co-workers with Christ, and help in the expansion of God's kingdom by playing a specific role, as part of a larger body. If a car is designed to function on roads, it can only be successful when it functions according to the pattern of its design. Every manufacturer designs their products with specific functions and purpose in mind.[18] For that reason, our attitude to service should stem from what we are designed to achieve.

As a Christian Musician & Singer:

---

[18] Munroe, *"The Purpose and Power of Praise & Worship."*

- ✓ I am designed to minister to God. To be effective for this design, I should have the relevant customer service skills that my client (God) looks out for.
- ✓ I am designed to minister to God's people. Therefore, I cannot have a lousy attitude, and must comport myself on and off duty.
- ✓ I am designed to WORK as a partner with God. Hence, I should be found in my duty post at the right time, as and when due.
- ✓ I am designed to be a support to the Pastoral Team, and not designed to be consistently at loggerheads with the Pastor as David was to Saul, and as the Minstrel was to Elisha. Therefore, a helper should not be seen at war with the person you are called to help.

Going by the first design, as Prophet and Worship Leader, constant communion with God is paramount. Isaiah makes this clear when he declares that:

> 'The Lord God has given Me the tongue of the learned,
> That I should know how to speak a word in season to him who is weary.
> He awakens me morning by morning,
> He awakens my ear to hear as the learned.'
>
> —Isaiah 50: 4

As a vessel with a message, the songs rendered to God and to his Saints should be songs at the appropriate seasons. This feat is accomplished by a life daily controlled by God. Hence, the choir or Worship Team is not a unit for those who join for the wrong reasons. These can include a desire for fame, a place where one can be paid in other to make ends meet, a place to make friends or find a spouse, or perhaps because you have a good voice. **It is a priesthood!** It is a place of calling, a place of service, a place of devotion, a place of consecration, a place of sacrifice and hard-work. In Acts 8: 9—24, we notice that like Simon the Sorcerer, some who appear to desire the anointing and the gifts of God do so for insincere reasons.

As a result, choristers and musicians should be vetted by the leadership of the Church. The vetting process is done by formal and informal auditions and interviews. Afterwards it is advisable to follow with a training or induction scheme, and those who are finally confirmed after their periods of probation should be developed and equipped for the sensitive role and duty required by that office. This is not far-fetched and too much to ask for. You may notice that appointment of singers and musicians in David's era was carried out by David himself and the leaders of the Levites.[19] This same principle is repeated by Jehoshaphat when Judah was to go to battle against the Moabites, Ammonites and the people of Mount Seir.[20]

It is noteworthy also to state that, in the current dispensation of grace, Paul reminds us that we are soldiers of the cross of Christ.

---

[19] See, *1 Chronicles 25: 1*
[20] See *2 Chronicles 20: 21*

> *'You therefore must endure hardship as a good soldier of Jesus Christ. ⁴ No one engaged in warfare entangles himself with the affairs of this life, that he may please him who enlisted him as a soldier.'*
>
> —2 Timothy 2: 3—4

As in the days of Jehoshaphat, and to this day, the Worship precedes warfare, as every service is a battleground between God and his opponents. We enter into God's gates with thanksgiving and access his courts through praise.[21] This is why it is recommended that those who lead worship and sing and play in the choir should be selected and appointed by trust within a framework that involves the leadership of the church. If these principles are followed, it helps to minimise the challenges associated with choirs, musicians and worship leaders and further provides a conducive platform for productivity in ministry.

---

[21] See *Psalm 100*

CHAPTER 2

The Dynamics of 'Corporate' Worship

Therefore, let him who speaks in a tongue pray that he may interpret. For if I pray in a tongue, my spirit prays, but my understanding is unfruitful. What is the conclusion then? I will pray with the spirit, and I will also pray with the understanding. I will sing with the spirit, and I will also sing with the understanding. Otherwise, if you bless with the spirit, how will he who occupies the place of the uninformed say "Amen" at your giving of thanks, since he does not understand what you say?
—*1 Corinthians 14: 13—16*

There have been so many family gatherings where my sister would tell my parents and my younger brothers the story of how my pocket money would finish at the first week of each semester in our undergraduate days. My father in particular would always burst out laughing at the punchline to her story which was her solution to this dilemma. Now, in order to unmask this problem from its root, she began to observe me very closely to find a way to deter the situation. She then tells us what she came to notice over time. Iyefu had discovered that I had a tendency to defer spending for as long as possible, if the currency available to me were fresh mint. I had a liking for very clean notes. So, from that moment onwards, she and my dad took it upon themselves to ensure I only got cash in fresh mints.

Whenever the *gist* came to this story, everybody apart from me found it funny and I never understand why. Still, even though I hardly ever enjoy the account in its entirety, I would still take part in the conversation in an attempt to shape the story from my own perspective. If you ask me, I think my sister always gave them an incomplete version of the chronology of events, and every time the tale was told, they would all burst out in laughter– leaving me very little opportunity to chip in my bit. Now, as the writer of the story, I get a chance to share with my readers more details about my sister's incomplete depiction of my student life.

As accurate as Iyefu's account of my spending habit was, a few details were never taken into consideration. As an undergraduate student, a good proportion of my pocket money went into the acquisition of books, cassette tapes, videos and CDs of my favourite preachers and gospel artists. As far as my sister, Iyefu was concerned, my priorities were misplaced, but for me, those resources were non-negotiable investments, especially as I had the longer term returns in view. Another point of consolation, in my defence boils down to the fact that, to this day, I nurse the habit of enjoying my own company. I never get bored of locking myself up in the room if there's a book to read, music or sermon to listen to or a video to watch. The times I would forget to eat in my *incommunicado moments* might number above a million and every now and then, those around me would come to check if I was okay, never understanding why I could spend so much time alone.

The prevailing point to the story is this— was it really her business at what point my money would run out or on what item it was used for? As I saw it, how I spent my money wasn't really Iyefu's business.

Then and again it was, because, by the second or third week of the semester, I would run to her or to my elder brother making a demand that required their financial support. So in one way or the other, my compulsive spending habit had its effect on my siblings.

Corporate worship is no different. What you do in the place of worship when alone should typically affect you alone. On the other hand, when worship involves two or more people, it can be a totally different pack of cards. As I mentioned earlier on, my obsession for the acquisition of Christian resources and materials had more positive effects in the grand scheme of things. As a starting point, it offered me a wider range in the number of songs I could sing or teach to a choir or congregation. It was easier for me to fit into any Christian circle without the fear of missing out in the worship experience. It was a booster in the place of relevance in God's vineyard, and lastly, I also discovered that like scriptures, the Holy Spirit only brings to your remembrance the amount of the Word (in this case, songs) already deposited in you. Still, as far as spending was concerned, I had to make realistic changes to lessen the inconvenience that could affect others around me in spite of what my personal preferences and indulgences were.

This brings me to the central point of this chapter and how this is distinguished from the points made previously. In the first chapter, we rightly identified God as the primary recipient of praises, worship and thanksgiving. Also, we recognised God to be the focal point of the worship. As a result, praise-worship is not designed to impress men, since the Heavenly audience supersedes the earthly congregation and any applause man can give. Regardless, where taken out of context relevant principles which should guide our worship experience can be misunderstood. You may have come across musicians and singers who show insensitivity to other worshipers simply because they believe only God (the recipient of the worship) matters.

There is a principle of cooperation required in public worship. In the privacy of one's home or at one's private altar, one may decide to sing off beat, in any and every key, in any language, with whatever style or format as one chooses. In corporate worship, the dynamics are invariably different. There are other considerations to be factored in. The word 'corporate' originates from 15th century Latin; *corporatus* translated to mean, *'to form into a body.'* If we go to the Oxford dictionary, this term refers to *anything shared by all the members* of a group. It connotes corporation and a collective responsibility to perform a certain exercise, role or function. From this angle, the dynamics of corporate worship involves two or more people. With that in view, members of a choir are expected to understand how a personal time of devotion is different from a public and collective time of worship. Both require the act of worship done in spirit and in truth to God.

Yet the format plays differently and depends on the individuals involved. For example, in my private devotion alone with God, I am at liberty to sing in any language. I could start off by singing the first stanza of a popular hymn in English, and jump abruptly to Spanish,

Swahili, or Swedish in the chorus of the song. However, as soon, as another child of God joins me to worship, I am obligated to pay attention to the new dynamics of the worship. The language may become limited to one understood by both of us. One of us may be skilled in music and the other may not. If that is the case, it may be better to limit the choices of songs to simple songs. Furthermore, if the worship occurs in a facility where hymn books are available or at a time and place where the lyrics of the songs are displayed, then one may sing —

> '*Over the mountains and the sea*
> *Your river runs with love for me,*
> *And I will open up my heart,*
> *And let the healer set me free.*
> *I'm happy to be in the truth,*
> *And I will daily lift my hands,*
> *And I will always sing of*
> *When your love came down, yeah.*'[22]

On the other hand, if the meeting point is at a home group[23], or a time of worship in a vehicle on a road trip where there are obviously no screens and projectors to facilitate help with the lyrics of songs, understanding and sensitivity are required. At such instances, whoever takes the lead is expected to pay attention to the ability of the others to sing along in worship to God. Choices of songs can be limited choruses that are common and easy to remember.

---

[22] Martin Smith, *I Could Sing of Your Love Forever*, Curious? Music/UK/Kingsway? Thankyou Music, 1994. CD
[23] Or *House Fellowship, House Cell*

This view is supported in scriptures. The book of Genesis offers pointers to the fact that certain individuals worshipped God privately. Noah is an example of an individual who worshipped God alone. Albeit, the first corporate worship recorded in scripture occurs between Abraham and Isaac.[24] Here Abraham observes God's instruction and takes his son yonder to worship God. When Isaac could not sight any item for sacrifice, he sought for answers, and Abraham assured him that God was going to make provision for the sacrifice. After Abraham had passed God's test, and a lamb was miraculously spotted by Isaac, we notice communication again. Isaac immediately communicated the change of plans to Abraham and their worship of God became a well-done joint effort. Next, we also notice Moses, Miriam and the Children of Israel worship with a song, tambourines and a dance in Exodus 15 after they had successfully crossed the Red Sea. Ron Kenoly points out that this collective worship between Moses, Miriam and the children of Israel was somewhat informal, whereas the choir set up by David in 1 Chronicles was one done formally for God's collective worship by God's people[25].

By that accounting, this chapter will pay attention to some of the key concepts of corporate worship, whether formal or informal. I call this the ABCD of corporate worship, discussed below in reverse order: "

---

[24] See *Genesis 22: 1—14*. Here Abraham offers up Isaac as a living sacrifice, and Isaac offers up himself.
[25] Ron Kenoly, *The Effective Praise and Worship Leader*, (Tabor: Parsons Publishing, 2008), 70

- Approach
- Bearings (gathering point)
- Communication
- Decency & Order.

Decency & Order

The first point of consideration in a worship involving more than one Christian believer is the line of order. *Who does what?* In Paul's first letter to the church in Corinth, they are instructed and admonished to be orderly in church.[26] First, Paul picks on divided labour and addresses diversities in calling, gifting and graces.[27] That is to say, someone may be responsible for the worship, another responsible for the teaching, another responsible for interpretation, etcetera. *'For God is not a God of disorder but of peace, as in all the meetings of God's holy people.'* — 1 Corinthians 14: 33 (NLT)

Secondly, he hints on a structure by his disapproval of disorder. This means that, in corporate worship, we work within a framework of organisation: a session for psalms and hymns (*which is what we may term 'praise worship' in modern contemporary church culture*), a session for teaching, a session for prayers, and a session for ministry. The point raised here focuses on decency and order, and not on routine and rigidity.

---

[26] *1 Corinthians 14: 26—40.*
[27] *1 Corinthians 12: 12—30 and 1 Corinthians 14: 26—27.*

Thirdly, Paul hints on the length and duration. If there is to be a session for psalms and hymns and another for teaching through divided labour, it then means that each aspect of the worship service is equally expected to have a time frame, so each person knows when they are expected to function. Paul further confirms the role of time keeping in corporate worship in his letter to the Church in Corinth. *'Remember that people who prophesy are in control of their spirit and can take turns.'* — 1 Corinthians 14: 32 (NLT)[28]

In other words, order in a service is produced by defining three elements:

- *Who leads?*
- *Who does what?*
- *What is the duration and length?*

Although there is nothing necessarily wrong if everybody is allowed to chip in when we sing choruses in a less formal setting, in many cases where that is the case, it can be quite ineffective or confusing. We are clearly told that God is not the author of confusion.[29] Imagine, I sing '*here I am to worship, here I am to bow down, here I am to say that you're my God*', and the brother standing or sitting next to me throws in a different song before we finish the current song. For instance, let's assume he then sings, '*Give thanks with a grateful heart, give thanks to the Holy One, give thanks because He's given Jesus Christ His Son*'

---

[28] The NKJV: 'And the spirits of the prophets are subject to the prophets.'
[29] 1 Corinthians 14: 33, loc. cit.

Then just before we all join in the chorus— '*And Now Let the Weak Say I Am Strong*', the sister next to him throws in a different song on a different key, and at a faster pace, '*We Wanna See Jesus Lifted High– A Banner That Flies Across This Land…*' such a scenario paints a picture of disorder.

David must have observed the importance of divided labour, structure and order. Hence, this led him to setup a specific group of skilled Levites who were then charged with the responsibility to lead the worship segments in corporate gatherings of God's people.[30] The angle of skill and expertise will be discussed in details in the following chapter.

Next, when worship is arranged in an orderly fashion, it is expected that the question of who does what is answered. Again, the sort of meeting in question also plays a role in the organisation of roles and responsibilities. For instance, if instruments such as drums, guitars, keyboards, and the piano and sound equipment are used, we should expect a sort of arrangement over who plays or operates on each of these instruments. This is the reason why most churches entrust the duty of leading the worship to a specific group of individuals commonly known as the choir, the worship team or other names synonymous to these two.

---

[30] See *1 Chronicles 25: 1* and *1 Chronicles 25: 7*. Attention is drawn to the calibre of those chosen: **Skilled**!

Therefore, those who are called and entrusted to oversee the music or the sound should strive to be faithful stewards in the office to which they have been called and assigned.[31] For example, sound engineers should not be late to meetings where their services are required. A worship leader whose duty is first on the agenda of an event should not be late to such a meeting. The keyboardist or violinist who helps with the key of the songs is expected to be on time, except under extenuating circumstances. More so, the moment people who serve in any of these capacities notice that they have to be unavoidably absent; they are expected to let someone with the ability to do something about it aware. In that way, arrangements can be made for temporal replacements or reorganisation of the programme.

Also, the members of the worship team should function in their respective offices. For example, we recognise that the drummer helps to regulate the tempo and time signatures for the music. If this is the case, if the drummer fails to be on his drum at the right time, then we should question the level of his or her effectiveness in their place of calling. It is not enough to be early to church, and then found at the corner of the church doing something else when the praise worship is about to start. Another example is a scenario where the drummer has no drum sticks or might have forgotten it at home. That points to an issue with preparation. It is uncommon or rather unusual for the preacher to forget his Bible. For effectiveness and efficiency, we expect that faithful stewards are available to function in their places

---

[31] See *Ephesians 4: 1*.

of assignment, teachable and prepared always. If the praise worship starts at 10am on Sunday morning, a keyboardist who remembers at 9.57am that the sustain pedal is still in the boot of his car can be more efficient. Efficiency would mean that you are on your instruments at least about 5 minutes before; adequately prepared, ready and on time.

Communication

As far as communication goes, there are two broad categories of communication:

- ✓ Intrapersonal Communication
- ✓ Interpersonal Communication

The first is internal, and the latter is external. Communication carried out internally does not involve anybody else. For example, when you imagine things, or think a thought and laugh out loud. Someone standing close by may wonder what could be so amusing to make you laugh out loud. It could be a conversation you played in your head that can remain unexpressed. Also when a person sleeps and dreams, at such a point, such a person is engaged in intrapersonal communication. If it is a bad dream, you might see such an individual turning or screaming, or making a conversation in their sleep.

Lastly, para-language is another form of intrapersonal communication. These can be manifested in different ways to include, yawning when one is tired or sleepy; a belch to indicate dehydration and a need to drink plenty of water, or even one's dressing to indicate moods, occasions, and events. If someone wears pyjamas to the church or office, that can indicate a serious mental problem, except if it was a pyjama party. When we see you in a towel, we immediately assume you might want to take a shower or might have just had one. If you decide to fix a problem with a vehicle, you might have to change from a white shirt and tie to something more appropriate for fixing engines and tyres. Paralanguage and body language are also forms of communication that delivers a message to others without formal oral expressions. Thus intrapersonal communication can be observed through one of the following:

- Paralanguage
- Body Language
- Body Impulse (coughing, yawning)
- Abstract forms of communication to include dreams, imaginations, internal dialogues, monologue.
- Dressing

On the other hand, interpersonal communication is expressed through some of the following:

- Speech
- Writing
- Sign Language
- Body Language
- Paralanguage

- Music
- Language, Dialects, Accents and Tone

Everyday humans communicate a message to others formally and informally. For example, when you look at your wrist watch, it could indicate to the other person a need to hurry up or round off the conversation. When you are late to a meeting and still catwalk or stroll in, that may indicate insensitivity towards the feeling of others and a narcissistic sense of self importance. It could also hint at negligence or hint at the significance of the meeting in question. All these elements are critical in corporate worship. This is because two or more cannot work together except there is some sort of agreement[32]. If two or more people are to magnify and exalt God together as a corporate entity, there has to be communication between the parties concerned.

Firstly, what language(s) are messages conveyed by? In the United States, songs can be written and sang mainly in English, African-American vernacular, and Spanish. The use of one, two or all of these languages has the power to include or exclude participation. For example, I may feel more comfortable and at ease in a fellowship where English is the primary language of communication. This is because, no matter how scripture based a song is in Spanish, or how anointed the songs are, I may be unable to worship accordingly as a result of my limitation in understanding that language. Do we then

---

[32] *Amos 3:3*

suppose or encourage separation where one only fellowships among people of the same language? No. Not necessarily. What Paul teaches is that he that speaks in an unknown tongue should provide an interpreter. Noting the compelling nature of Apostle Paul's teaching, songs outside the official lingua franca should be translated for the benefit of a wider audience.

In England, English is notably the official and popular language of communication. However, with the cosmopolitan structure of places like London, we find that people from various ethnicities and countries from all over the world who become a part of the diaspora, come together to fellowship among themselves. These can include, and are not limited to the following; the Chinese, Congolese, French, Ghanaians, Greeks, Portuguese, Nigerians, Southern Africans, among many others.

Regardless of whatever ethnicities, persuasions, or majority exist in the church, it has to be treated as the body of Christ, which is open to anyone who believes in God.

Undoubtedly, in corporate worship, attention has to be paid to understanding. We pray in the spirit, but also pray in understanding. We sing in the spirit, and also sing in understanding.[33] When I do not understand the language choice of the choir's selection of songs, it might mean that all is yet to be done to effect corporate

---

[33] *1 Corinthians 14: 13—16.*

worship in that meeting. For this reason, the worship leader must be sensitive to lead the congregation with the relevant communication skills required to be effective. And this begins with language and translations.

Secondly, the tools of communication are equally important in corporate worship. For example, the right language might be in place, and yet, people may still find it difficult to pick out what the singer is saying. This is why the use of visual aids such as the projector and projector screens, song sheets, a bulletin or a hymn book is pivotal. The worship leaders should not be seen enjoying themselves while the rest of us wonder what exactly they just sang. It is also important for singers to enunciate and pronounce words clearly. Sometimes when the worship leader complains over a cold response, it might be that the mechanisms to carry the people along are not in place. When you play your part by ensuring, the congregation have an idea of what you are saying, and you also ensure that they have the lyrics, meaning and understanding of the message(s) made available, then every other aspect is likely to fall in line.

Thirdly, 'when in Rome', it is okay to be Roman. When in France, being American might not do much good. For the fact a song is popular in Louisiana or Arizona does not necessarily mean an imitation of the exact accent and the precise *ad lib* of the original American singer will be as effective in London and in Accra. People, in general, expect a level playing field in corporate worship. A worship leader who listens to Kirk Franklin or Byron Cage, and then decides to use the exact same words of admonition, same accent and all, lacks originality. I am even told that there have been instances where the language of the Holy Spirit spontaneously spoken in a CD recording was copied verbatim by some soloists during a repeat performance! By all means, be at liberty to be imitators of that which is good, as long as it is done within reasonable limits.

Fourthly, para and body languages are critical features in effective worship leading. From experience, people respond better to a believable product. If God is good, then prove it. As a worship leader, does your facial expression and body language match your claim? Your facial expression can sometimes be a giveaway in successfully carrying out your assignment to lead the congregation in the Worship of God. If the drummer is getting on your nerves and you make it obvious by your body language, there are some people in the congregation who might pick the body language signal. A smile is usually a very effective body language, and the joy of the Lord and that inner peace and sincerity can also help the choir and Worship Leader.

Then there is also the aspect of dressing and appearance. As a Christian singer or musician, you will have to decide what your objectives are. Motives should be scrutinised. Self-examination and evaluation should be carried out. Does the dress make me stand out? Is it too loud? Does it draw unnecessary attention to me, or does it portray the image of Christ? Am I underdressed? Am I looking shabby? Am I moderate? Am I well-groomed? Am I neat and tidy? Am I decent? As a Christian lady, it should go without saying that the image of Christ is at the centre of how you appear. Furthermore, for men and women alike, indecent exposure of cleavages, undergarments, and body parts can be a distraction to somebody else.

While, it is argued that God is not concerned with a man's outward appearance, it is significantly important that such scripture is put in the right context. That scripture was borne out of a conversation between God and Samuel, prior to the ordination of David as King of Israel. In the right context, while Samuel looked at the stature of Jesse's son, God was more interested in someone whose heart was pure before Him. Within that context, God is impartial; he can use anybody who makes themselves available irrespective of social class, background, education, looks, and pedigree. That scripture has nothing to do with indecent and irresponsible dressing. Paul supports this notion in his thesis on the law of liberty and its limitations in the 14th chapter of the book of Romans.[34] Furthermore, God specifically uses dressing as a symbol of purity. He asserts that the Bridegroom is coming for a bride whose garment is without spot or wrinkle.[35] Hence, distractions must be brought to the minimum, as much as possible.

Bearing (Location)

Location can also affect the dynamics of corporate worship in different ways. For example, if the worship is to take place on the bus, on a road trip, a sound system, a microphone and a keyboard may

---

[34] See *Roman 14: 1—3*, and *Romans 14: 15—21*.
[35] Also see *Zechariah 3: 1—3*.

be unnecessary or impractical. Conversely, in a meeting of more than 100 people, it may be difficult to hear the singer at the front without the use of a microphone. Accordingly, this has to be factored in the plan and structure of a corporate gathering.

Worship leaders and musicians are also expected to consider the acoustics and ambience of the venue. Singing in a cathedral changes the dynamics of vocal production, and so does singing in an enclosure, or open space. In putting up a repertoire of songs, attention should be paid to what is available. Are there musical instruments? If yes, what sort? Is there a microphone or do I have to project loud enough for others to hear? Is the music too loud in similarity to a disco hall or club where one strains to hear the ordinary voice? Bad sound can be off-putting. If the music is too loud, it can be hazardous and strenuous to the ears and unpleasant.

Hence, it stands to reason that those of us in the music team are expected to be a little more sensitive to our environment and sensitive to the congregation we lead. Experience has shown that investment in the training of sound engineers and the worship team help to provide a decent worship environment. If your church does not have a sound engineer, those who are trusted with the responsibility for sound management should be encouraged to attend seminars, read books and magazines on sound management, take lessons, and make profitable the gift that has been deposited inside of them. By so doing, corporate worship can be enhanced for the benefit of many, rather than a few.

Approach

Finally, in corporate worship, it is also necessary to consider an approach to the structure and church culture of each denomination or group of people. Even though we are one body in Christ, our approach and expressions may differ from one gathering to the other. A good example of this is demonstrated in Paul's letters to the churches. In his letter to the church in Galatia, Paul begins with a prayer for the church[36]. He was astonished at their swift backsliding and the many troubles that seemed to affect the church in Galatia at the time.[37] On the other hand, in his first and second letters to the church in Thessaloniki, Paul begins with thanksgiving. Their work of faith was outstanding and grew in an abounding measure, and their challenges as we read on are different to that of the churches in Galatia, Philippi and the others.

In the same vein, our approach to corporate worship may differ, one church to the other. You may appoint lead singers to lead at different segments of the service, while another may appoint a conductor who co-ordinates the start, dynamics and ending of a hymn sang in unison by everybody. What is crucial is that there is a structure and defined approach in the coordination of the worship service. I have been to services where the worship leaders sing from a song sheet with a stand in front, taking breaks in between each song. Whenever these breaks occur, it allows for people to pause and reflect on the meaning of the

---

[36] *Galatians 1: 3—7*
[37] *Ibid.*

song, and we find that it could also work out as an opportunity to transition into the next song on a different key.

Whereas singing from a song sheet in another church is perceived to be as a result of incompetence on the path of the lead singer. In some other churches, a break in between songs is sometimes perceived to be a break in the flow. When I was growing up, at our family morning devotions, everyone was permitted to lead in turns. Interestingly, it still worked out to be fairly decent and coordinated. I'm not sure how effective that may work in a church setting though. The crucial point is that we are to recognise the existence of variations in our approach to corporate worship and the coordination of the music or worship.

CHAPTER 3

The Element of Excellence in Corporate Worship

That you may approve the things that are excellent, that you may be sincere and without offense till the day of Christ.
—Philippians 1:10

As the completion of this book was fast approaching, I sat down pondering about any missing dynamics to the project, and then it occurred to me that it might be good to fish and chip in an awfully embarrassing experience of the past. Another decision I made on that note, was to pick out a story, which mainly involved me to protect other parties from a tell-it-all- story written without their consent. It also had to be one that I find relevant to the subject of discussion, and as I travelled across into the city of retrospection and reflection, the search for the right story appeared harder and harder to find. Eventually, I fell asleep, knowing I had a flight to catch in the morning. As a visitor in the city of New York, I didn't want to take any chances, by travelling on the metro on a day I had a morning flight from LaGuardia Airport to Dallas Forth Worth.

By 6.30am, I was up and almost ready to head to the Airport to catch my 10.30am flight to Dallas, with the mind to catch up with a friend who would drive us down to *Redemption Camp* in Greenville, Texas. After the usual daily routine, as soon as I jumped into the cab, I noticed the driver was a jolly good fellow. He was a fairly young good looking man probably around his early or mid-thirties.

More often than not, whenever I entered into a cab, I would utter a pleasant greeting and ask the driver how he was, and how his day had so far, been. Then with attentive ears, I would internally attempt to decipher his geographical background, religious ethos, his possible educational and social background, before jumping into a conversation if I was in the mood for a chat. On this day, I wasn't really in the mood, and this had nothing to do with the pressure to get to the airport on time. I set out more than two and half hours early for a trip that I envisaged would take about approximately 30 minutes without traffic.

Thanks to Google, I had already been briefed on the specific terminal and gate number, I had checked in online, I had no bags to physically check in, and furthermore, Google had hinted the traffic routes and the traffic free routes. Hence, all that I cared about was to get to the airport in record time and to find the right icebreaking story for a chapter of my book. As I sat in the taxi listening to the boring stories the driver told, given that I was inattentive, and totally removed from whatever it was he was saying, I confirmed that the stories I believe the Holy Spirit had brought to my remembrance the previous day and night were the relevant and applicable ones to be shared.

So I begin, with an incident that occurred while I was an undergraduate student at the University of Jos. The General Overseer of the Redeemed Christian Church of God (RCCG), made a decision to hold the Ministers and Workers' Conference of the year in two locations. Originally, everyone had to go to Lagos, but on this occasion, the GO as we call him, was coming to Jos, at a time when I happened to be a student there. It was exciting news, and even more interesting was that I had been given the opportunity to lead the Worship on the opening night of the conference. I took time out to fast, pray and to prepare to be a part of what God had planned to do in the meeting. After every praise worship session, I could more often than not, tell if I thought I had successfully carried out my assignment. In my estimation, and as it seemed to appear, I believe I had given my best.

After the worship, the GO was ushered to take his seat and proceed with the business of the evening. As he approached where a seat and a table had been reserved for him, he picked up the microphone and said, 'let somebody shout hallelujah!' We all chorused a shout of hallelujah in elation. Afterwards, he knelt down and led the congregation in a song, while I and the other singers joined in as backing vocals to the GO. Prior to his coming, we had been victims of a religiously incited riot against the Christians in the city. As a result, a curfew had been originally imposed from dusk to dawn, leaving me and my brother house bound at the initial start of the riot. This was later reduced to a curfew that would begin sometime around 4pm till 5am in the morning for security reasons. For the Church in Jos, we were no longer sure if the Ministers Conference would still hold. However, the GO had told our State Pastor, as we called him, that the Conference would go on, and that God would step in before the date in question.

At precisely a few days before the General Overseer's arrival, the curfew was moved to 12am till 4am, which then implied that we could carry on with the planned conference. Anyone who has ever been subject to a curfew or stuck at an unwanted location for any reason may understand why we were extremely excited. It was a double celebration, to have the General Overseer in the city, and to be part of something that was historic. In my naivety and excitement, I failed to pay careful attention to the words of an introductory song he taught.

The words, went this way:

> 'The works of Thy hands magnify Thee
> The Angels in Heaven sing Thy praise
> And all we Saints together sing,
> Blessed be Thy name, blessed be Thy name.'[38]

As I accompanied in the singing, with a loud voice, I sang, '*Thy works of Thy hands magnify Thee…*' Being a meticulous teacher, the GO paused the singing and gave myself and the congregation I must have misled an English lesson. He said in his soft and very pleasant baritone, '*My English might not be very good, but I remember my teacher had taught us that when "the" is used before a vowel, it is pronounced "thuh" and when it comes before a consonant it is pronounced "thee". So the is "thuh works of Thy hands", so let's take it again".*

---

[38] Author unknown

I knew without any doubt that I was the culprit, even more so, it was recorded on video and in audio cassette, so there could be no question of who in the choir had sung the incorrect word. Today, I'm so glad that, he was meticulous enough to correct me, even though he did so lovingly and without making it obvious who the culprits were. To that effect, I learnt to pay diligent attention to the lyrics of every song, and also try to ensure, I understand and interpret each song within the appropriate context. This is what excellence does. It pays attention to details and seeks to promote the very good standard and good value to an element.

On that note, you may have noticed that when excellence in the worship ministry is discussed, it is often misunderstood and somewhat controversial. In order to explore the reason why this happens to be the case, you may have to establish what excellence is. As a verb, 'excel' means to be exceptionally good or outstanding in an activity or subject[39]. Hence, excellence has to do with the quality and outcome of (in this case) the worship. Daniel is notably remembered as a man with the spirit of excellence. He excelled above his contemporaries to the point of envy and jealousy. He represented God alright by his outstanding performance and became a force to be reckoned with in his time.[40] Yet, when excellence is discussed as far as worship is concerned, we find that there are some who equate excellence with

---

[39] Catherine Soanes and Sara Hawker (ed), *Oxford English Dictionary for Students*, (Oxford: Oxford University Press, 2006), 345
[40] See *Daniel 6:3*.

carnality. What should be typically unacceptable in music is tolerated within church walls.

One reason to explain this phenomenon can be as a result of the fact that in modern Christian practice, as Ron Kenoly refreshingly puts it; most choirs are informal and are made up of people without formal music training and experience.[41] As part of the ripple effect, people are allowed to join the choir without formal auditions and in some cases, they are allowed to join without any genuine ability to sing or play an instrument well. Even when auditions are carried out, some leaders do it to fulfil all righteousness. There is no set criteria and yardstick to determine who makes the auditions in question. Everyone scales through! When that occurs, it becomes a challenge and sometimes difficult to deliver an exceptionally good production.

Another reason why the subject of excellence can be a little controversial is that people can be a bit edgy when it appears their worship to God is being analysed or put to scrutiny and examination. If my praise and worship is an offering to God, then why should anyone else care if I missed the words, had a bad start or perhaps failed to modulate with the music?

The answer has been partly elaborated in chapter two: - Private worship is none of our business. Corporate worship is! As a choir, you have a dual responsibility to God and the congregation.[42] Christopher

---

[41] Kenoly, *"The Effective Praise and Worship Leader."*
[42] See *Hebrews 6:10*

J Ellis phrases it in a remarkable fashion; he asserts that as a worship leader you need to worship with three eyes, an eye for the congregation, a second eye should focus on God and a third eye on the clock.[43] If a woman prepares a meal for her husband, and for their guests, it then means that the perception of the quality of that meal is no longer open to her husband alone, but to every other person who tastes of the food. The husband is expected to appreciate the effort that has gone into the cooking more than anyone else. It doesn't matter if an ingredient is missing, or if the salt was a little overboard. Courtesy demands appreciation for her efforts. However, the other partakers in the meal may not be as generous with their compliment.

In contrast, when people have had a good meal, they might comment on how delicious it was. In a similar fashion, as a worship leader, we can agree that God is the bridegroom and ultimate recipient of the worship. Everyone else who is part of the worship experience may have a thing or two to say also, whether good or bad. From that standpoint, there are substantial reasons why excellence should be given a level of attention at our worship gatherings.

- Deep calls to deep [It is designed for the most excellent being] – Psalm 42: 7
- God commands it (Psalm 66: 2, Ecclesiastes 9: 10)

---

[43] Christopher J. Ellis, *Approaching God: A Guide for Worship Leaders & Worshipers*, (Canterbury: Canterbury Press, 2009), 9-11.

- Minimises distractions for the benefit of the congregation (Philippians 1:10)
- Provides a yardstick to weight productivity and progress
- Demonstrates God's excellence and glory for the world to see.

We should also remember that the pursuit of excellence in our delivery is hinged on association with the author of excellence. Worship and songs to be presented to God should be well done, and well presented. The reason is simple:

- *God is excellent!*
- *His name is excellent (Psalm 8:1)*
- *His loving-kindness is excellent and second to none (Psalm 36:7).*
- *God is excellent in greatness (Psalm 150: 2)*
- *God is excellent in power, judgement and justice (Job 37: 23)*
- *God is excellent in working (Isaiah 28: 29)*
- *God has done excellent things which is evidenced by the mystery of creation (Isaiah 12: 5)*

Even his angels excel in strength, and his Spirit is the Spirit of excellence. Consequently, it follows that services rendered to an excellent God should be exceptionally good. A good analogy to illustrate this position is the principle of reciprocity. This doctrine is practised in diplomatic relations all over the world. Basically, reciprocity is a universally accepted principle of international law also applied in international relations where a State adopts a given behaviour symmetrical in response to that adopted by another State.[44] This means that if God's gifts to you are exceptionally good and outstanding, your offerings (worship) to him should be exceptionally good and outstanding in return.

As a consequence, it then means that effort should be made to perfect the arrangements of the music at every opportunity made available to the worship team. In addition, as a worship leader, singer or musician, Paul recommends that we approve the things which are excellent.[45] In other words, you should also take the steps necessary to ensure an outstanding delivery always. Bear in mind that when musicians and singers are given the task of leading worship week after week, it becomes a routine for some and further desensitises and demotivates them from putting their best in the task of leading God's people to the throne room. When this occurs, complacency and laxity might slip in unnoticed. Familiarity, as they say, breeds contempt! The vigour and diligence may diminish over time. This accounts for the late coming to rehearsals, which could in turn result in a late rehearsal start and an inability to perfect the songs in some cases. For some others, they may be physically present at the rehearsal and emotionally and psychologically detached from what is going on, in the physical. Then on the day of delivery, they mix the words, startle or fail to give their best.

---

[44] Osheen Ishmael. *'Reciprocity in International Relations' Notes On Diplomatic Practices*. (2013): 41. Accessed October 25 2015. https://odeenishmaeldiplomacy.wordpress.com/2013/08/19/41-reciprocity-in-international-relations/
[45] *Philippians 1: 10*

The second reason why there has to be a conscious effort at excellence in the worship is that God commands it. We see this in Ecclesiastes 9: 10 where it states that *'Whatever your hand finds to do, do it with your might; for there is no work or device or knowledge or wisdom in the grave where you are going.'*[46] A wise saying goes; whatever is worth doing is worth doing well. The sentiment expressed in these quotes embodies the view that, anything short of excellence is inconsistent with what God commands in Psalms 66:2, Ecclesiastes 9:10 and in Colossians 3: 23. When you serve God, he expects a good job. Some might wonder if there's any such thing as a good job or bad job in the service of God. Yes, there is. A good illustration to paint the picture of what excellence is and what it is not can be easily pointed out from the popular television shows, the *X-Factor*, or the *American Idol* where the excellent make it to the finals, and the mediocre provide a good laugh at the beginning of the show. Have you ever heard people sing, where they leave you in a state of embarrassment on their behalf? Have you ever been in that position where you can't wait for the moment of ear torture to be over, because the song itself becomes a form of noise pollution? And when this happens in church, sometimes we are obliged to at least clap our hands in applause for the effort put into the rendition.

If you ever watched the movie, *Sister Act*, you might remember that the moment the Choir began to put effort and the right structure and detail to their singing, those who had left the church began

---

[46] NLT, Also in *Colossians 3: 23*

to return, and in no time their fame spread abroad. Even the Pope was moved to come and hear the Nuns sing when excellence and innovation were introduced to their delivery. Although this example is based on a fictional story, it bears a resemblance to the true state of things in reality. Excellence attracts, and mediocrity repels. Success, as someone says, has many brothers; whereas failure, on the other hand, is an orphan.

Thirdly, excellence also minimises distraction. Imagine when the worship is intense, hands are lifted to God in surrender, some are on their knees in deep contrition, and then the worship leader goes off tangent, maybe the microphone feedbacks an ugly sound, or perhaps the singer enters a new song on the wrong key at the wrong time, or struggles to be in alignment with the pace of the drums, and in one sweep of the moment, you quickly find yourself back on earth, you open your eyes as a result of the distraction, and then try to reconnect again, and the moment is lost. For people who are experienced, they may find ways to remain unperturbed from whatever is not going well with the music or in the choir. However, there are new believers or people in the congregation who can be lost as a result. For that reason, Choristers are encouraged to make an effort at keeping mistakes to the barest minimum, and that only comes by due diligence in one's area of calling.

There's also a further point to be considered; this is similar to the first point where attention is focused on the thread of connection between an excellent God and his associates. This time, aside from the importance of reciprocity, we offer excellent services in order to represent God as his ambassadors. Bad singing in church paints a negative picture of what God is all about. People may not be able to sing professionally. However they have access to music video channels on cable television, the internet, *YouTube*, *Spotify*, *iTunes* and so many different avenues to listen to very well done music. When they come to church and meet the opposite, it under-represents God who should be associated with excellence all round.

Next, it is equally important that a discourse that focuses on excellence within the Christian framework should aim to present a balance and possible exceptions to the rule. On that note, it is noteworthy to provide a little insight on the limits of excellence and how it can be measured and imbibed at Christian corporate gatherings.

First, excellence should be measured on the lens of manpower and capacity. That is to say, a church established and long standing may have a larger capacity of resources and manpower when compared to a new church start up. A pastor who expects a two—year old choir to produce a fantastic repetition of Richard Smallwood's *'Total Praise'* may be unrealistic and set a standard that is temporarily unattainable, in a situation where most of the existing members of the choir are new to the experience. They may lack the experience, time, and resources that were put together for a production of the song, 'Total Praise.' A reproduction of a song done by 100 experienced singers, may not sound as good when performed by ten people with a significantly lower experience in music.

Where this is the case, it is important to access the level where your team really is, and then set targets and put systems in place to push to a higher level of excellence. This may require additional training that is led by an experienced music instructor and worship leader. It may also require investments in the worship ministry. For example, some keyboards sound better than others. If the keyboard or technical instruments used in a church is of very low quality, the chances are that it could also affect the productivity of the choir. Hence, these factors have to be put into consideration in our assessment of how well a choir or worship team does.

Secondly, the vision of the church may also be another significant factor worthy of note. Some churches start up with a formidable choir at the onset, and some churches metamorphose into something big from a small start. The result of a church that begins as a house fellowship of two adults and three children may not be as great, as a church that begins with a 30 man-capacity choir. The Redeemed Christian Church of God is an example of a mission that began like a mustard seed and has grown in leaps and bounds. Moreover, with a vision to plant churches within a distance of fifteen minutes apart from other branches, you will find, that the choir may begin with a tiny fraction, which then grows over time.

Consequently, for churches where the choir may not be great from the start, excellence can be imbibed from one measure to another. One of the ways this goal can be achieved is by laying down certain rudiments in place. First among these, is to agree on what the target is. Model churches and choirs that may have already attained the level one hopes to attain can be visited. In addition to such visits, such groups can be studied. The scriptural authority for this model is seen in Hebrews 10: 24 where we are encouraged to *think of ways to motivate one another to acts of love and good works.*[47] Pastor Enoch Adeboye on occasions has made reference to his preliminary visit to South Korea. The miracles he witnessed in his early 80s visit to Seoul ignited a passion for a replication of God's miraculous move in his ministry. Today, we can attest to the fact that God has done much more in his ministry. This goes to show that when one presents an expectation through a model example of what you hope to achieve or accomplish, it sets the ball rolling. It is only those with a hunger who are filled. To acquire excellence, there has to be a hunger for excellence.

---

[47] (NLT)

CHAPTER 4
The Average Challenges of a Choir

Come to Me, all you who labour and are heavy laden, and I will give you rest. Take My yoke upon you and learn from Me, for I am gentle and lowly in heart, and you will find rest for your souls. For My yoke is easy and My burden is light.
—Matthew 11: 28-30

On my first day at St John's Church, I remember staring at the large clock attached to the brownish brick wall and if guesses counted for anything, this Church must have been built in the Victorian era. In some way, the setting reminded me of Maria's marriage to Captain Von Trapp in the *Sound of Music* film. I could hear the *thump thump* sound of my heartbeat—not minding the fact that as usual, I had prayed before leaving my studio apartment that evening. Sheffield was new terrain, and I had no idea what challenges to expect as the new Worship Director for the team my Pastor later named, *High Call*. New to the scene as it may have seemed, one fact was certain—there would be hurdles to cross, battles to fight, lessons to learn, friendships to be developed, and a never ending life of prayer to be made to the prayer-answering God.

Like Jerusalem and Rome, Sheffield is said to be built on seven hills and six rivers. Insofar as I was not in the city as a tourist, I paid little attention to the number of rivers in Sheffield while I lived there. Nonetheless, I hardly believe any resident or visitor to the steel city would deny coming across one or two hillsides. Of these hills, the one of Crooksmoor Road by far stands out the most to me. It is also nearly impossible to forget what it was like to walk up and down the road leading to St John's Church from the city centre. To begin with, they could count as good work-out sessions and they also paved way for good conversations whenever we walked that path in pairs. As parishioners approach the church seated at the centre of a land measuring around 130,000 square foot, they are greeted by the site of many beautiful trees as short as the English walnut and magnolia trees. The lawn is mowed, and the waft of spring rain signalled sweet sensations and serenity second to none.

When we stepped into the rehearsal room, I was glad that I was acquainted with at least one-third of the choristers already. This was different to my experience in Manchester, where I literally had to start from the scratch as far as relationships were concerned and because I only knew a handful of people the first time I joined the choir at their rehearsal, my reaction wasn't considered funny, to say the least. If you were in my shoes, you may have taken a similar position to me. What I observed, as far as I was concerned was shocking. First, we used a rehearsal studio at the heart of Deansgate. These kinds of studio are predominantly dark, enclosed and padded with noise proofs. There were no chairs in the room. All we had was three microphones with stands for each mic, and one amplifier for any guitars or instruments on the ground.

To my dismay, I watched as a 6'3-inch tall baritone was paired to a microphone stand with a 5'4-inch alto singer. It wasn't clear if she was making an effort to grow taller or if he was bending low enough to share the microphone with her. I found two things fundamentally wrong with the arrangement—the heights were incompatible to be paired together, and the parts they sang were different. To top it all, prior to my coming, some had no idea what a tenor and alto or soprano was. As I already mentioned, being much younger and immature, I'm not sure I handled the situation in a decent fashion. Moreover, my only friends who were as ingenuous as I was found the entire saga hilarious. One of them laughed out so loud in the middle of a tête-à-tête between us and this was very distracting and discouraging to the others, and even more to the leader of the team. Just like I mention at the start, it eventually worked out for good.

As Tessy and I stepped into the vicinity of St John's and to the rehearsal room—this time, I prepared to handle any shockers with wisdom and maturity. We were immediately greeted by the excitement in the air. As soon as this was over, I watched the team go into the business of the day, while I kept mute, only playing the role of a neutral observer. For the repeated time, I was utterly dumbfounded at the level of disorganisation, and impressed by the amazing potential of these talented and anointed group of young men and women. So, this time, I made mental notes of the challenges that was caught out for me—to succeed I would need a small team of partners to iron out the loopholes I had obviously identified in one clean swoop: administration, management, structure, discipline and discipleship.

Some of these loopholes showcase themselves as challenges many choirs deal with on a regular basis. And if you are familiar with the inner workings of church life, you should know that one of the most complex units in any church, ministry or religious based organisation is the choir[48]. It has been rightly called the 'hot-spot' or 'trouble zone.' As a result, a successful worship ministry has to be built on the foundation of constant prayers, a life of righteousness and practical weekly reviews. Besides, as with any noteworthy task, the build up of a successful choir comes with different possible challenges. Some of these challenges come up at different stages of ministry, in some cases, they are faced at the onset, and in other instances, they crop up as a result of expansion and church growth. The list below may not be exhaustive, but it covers some of the basic issues faced by some churches—

- Lack of Human Resources
- Lack of Adequate Music Facilities
- Lack of Dedicated Volunteers
- Lack of Motivation
- Lack of Understanding
- Lack of Discipline
- Finance
- Sound

---

[48] *Some churches use the term Choir regardless of the number of the ensemble. Others call theirs, a worship team or praise team. Then there are churches who employ the use of both terms, having a choir and a worship team with either a similar task or two separate tasks. In the video recording of Hillsong Australia's 'Shout to The Lord 2000' and in some other Hillsong Concerts, we notice the use of both a choir and a worship team. In this chapter, the term, choir refers to both.*

- People Management
- Conflict Resolution Methods

As stated above, inadequate human resources can pose a challenge to the success of a worship team. In an ideal situation, a successful worship ministry will require a set of musicians who play one instrument or the other, and a set of vocalists who sing. In Psalm 150: 3—5, we are instructed to praise God with diverse instruments. The harp and lyre, for instance, are string instruments that can help us regulate the key and tone we sing on in a corporate worship setting. Without the instruments that help unify our singing, our songs would be chaotic and very displeasing to listeners.

Some other instruments that help unify our tone are the trumpet, the saxophone, or keyboard. As humans, we mostly lack the ability to sing on the right note. In a practical scenario, imagine you come to church on a Sunday, and the first person who leads the prayer begins with a very uncomfortable key. You try to sing along and discover it is too high. You then try a lower octave and discover it is too low. It then happens that after their session of prayer, you have been given the task to lead the congregation in singing a hymn or songs of praise and worship. Imagine if there is no keyboard or instrument with the ability to help you pick a more comfortable key. You may struggle to find a suitable key on your own. And even when you do, someone who is tone deaf may out-sing you and change the key to something uncomfortable. Instruments are designed to help everybody fall in line. Such scenarios seldom occur when there is a brass, string, or wind instrument in the building.

The percussions (drums), also help to regulate the tempo and rhythm of the music. In their absence, people tend to start the song at different intervals, and in such scenarios, one could struggle all through the session. Although these are some of the reasons why it is more advisable to sing with accompanying instruments, it is important also to put it out that, the absence of music instruments may not always be a bad idea. Acapella is also an acceptable style of worship. In Western Africa, this style was in vogue in the 70s and 80s. It is still practised at gatherings that take place in a home set up. Nevertheless, it is not an ideal system in a corporate setting, because the Psalms tell us to praise God with the voice, with clapping of hands, and with as many instruments at our disposal. For this reason, where there is a lack of people to play relevant music instruments, it could present its own challenges.

Besides, on occasions, there could also be a lack of singers. I remember occasions where as a choir, we lacked Sopranos, Altos, and Tenors, at different seasons. You could always tell that something was missing, and the missing part puts a strain on those available. Where there are no Soprano singers, the Altos are forced to sing the melody and hit some notes that are naturally uncomfortable for their voice range. This could also happen in the reverse, where Sopranos are frustrated at the need to harmonise. Moreover, male and female singers are designed with different vocal abilities and a fusion of both in a choir, help to produce an appealing sound. In a church where male and female worship leaders are available, you can always tell the difference. They produce a variety which dispels potential boredom and excessive repetition.

As a consequence, a lack of human resources, in any of the aforementioned capacity, can be a challenge, especially in a church that has been exposed to good music internally or externally. It is not strange to go to another church, and wonder, 'why can't we have that in my church also?' The first answer to the absence of a keyboardist, bass player, drummer or singers is prayers. In Luke 10: 2 this is what Jesus had to say about insufficient hands.

> *'...The harvest is great, but the workers are few. So pray to the Lord who is in charge of the harvest; ask him to send more workers into his fields'* (NLT).

Sometimes, we think that an appeal to prayer is impractical and unrealistic. But if the truth is to be told, prayers should be the first response to a lack of human resources. Another reason why prayer is crucial is that, if the Lord of the Harvest sends in more volunteers to help in your worship team, the difference will always be much bigger than human effort. Furthermore, those who are sent by God tend to be a blessing to the group, and by and large, they become a blessing to the church. However, those who are not sent by God, constitute a problem for the leaders of the group and the leadership of the church. They could influence others negatively if care is not taken.

Turning now to the second action point, here is the approach Jesus used in his own time on earth. He fasted and prayed, and went out afterwards to pick his disciples. In some cases, God may require the leaders to go out to evangelise. In the process of evangelism, potential talents are discovered. Your drummer, for all we know, may not be one who is looking for greener pastures one church from the other. He or she may be on the street, and will only be found when you play your part in carrying the gospel of Jesus to those on the streets, the shopping centres, and those on the highways and the byways. At other times, it may require an announcement. Some of Jesus' disciples were not directly handpicked by Jesus, but by other disciples. In John 1: 45, Jesus reached out to Philip, and Philip reached out to Nathaniel. *Philip went to look for Nathanael and told him, "We have found the very person Moses and the prophets wrote about! His name is Jesus, the son of Joseph from Nazareth." (NLT).*

Another challenge similar to an insufficient number of helping hands is the lack of music facilities or an insufficient quantity or quality to accommodate the capacity of the church. While one church may lack human resources, another may lack instruments and public address systems that are of good quality. For some, the equipment available is mishandled by inexperienced or carefree volunteers. Shall we begin by addressing the function of music equipment and public address system for our worship services? Returning to the subject of corporate worship, where two or more people offer collective worship to God, the balance of necessity changes. In a gathering of 20 people, we can comfortably do without a microphone, but when we talk about 20 or more people, the responsibility to ensure that everyone is carried along within reason, falls on the church leadership. If microphones are to be used, it is advisable to purchase one of good quality. If a microphone that breaks intermittently is used, it could defeat the purpose of the gathering, distract people from paying attention or frustrate the worship experience. It makes more economic sense to purchase gadgets that are durable.

On the other hand, when these gadgets are purchased, those who act as stewards of God's resources are trusted with the task of providing due diligence in the place of management. When you buy a keyboard or drum kit, or a microphone or any instrument for that matter, choirs, musicians and sound engineers should ensure that they read the instruction manuals, and follow the rules for maintaining these instruments. Sometimes, gadgets are damaged as a result of mismanagement, and this should not be the case. God requires faithfulness in stewardship.[49]

We may now proceed to a third and fourth challenge faced by some churches: a lack of dedication and the lack of motivation. For some choirs, you find that very few are committed to the vision of the ministry they find themselves in. Where this is the case, absenteeism and late coming are visibly common factors among members of the team. The absence of commitment is caused by many factors; it could be as a result of a lack of understanding of purpose, or perhaps a lack

---

[49] See 1 Corinthians 4: 2. *Now, a person who is put in charge as a manager must be faithful (NLT).*

of motivation, or the inability to commit fully to serve, due to other commitments such as jobs, businesses, academics, family, and the likes. To put it in perspective, if I am meant to be a part of a church with the responsibility to serve in the choir, and I'm found to be inconsistent in dedication to my duties, there has to be a reason for it.

Thus, if the choir struggles with committed volunteers, a change will only be possible when the factors responsible for the absence of dedication is addressed. If you find that the main factor responsible for lack of commitment has to do with a lack of motivation or a lack of understanding of purpose, in such instances, it is the responsibility of leaders to correct that issue by providing relevant trainings that tackle the problems of motivation, and by also sharing and selling the vision to the team. In order to run with a vision, it has to be written in a language that is relatable, and it has to be read.[50] If you find musicians and singers who lack understanding of what their job and responsibility is, you cannot blame them, unless they have been told.

> *But how can they call to him for help if they have not believed? And how can they believe if they have not heard the message? And how can they hear if the message is not proclaimed? And how can the message be proclaimed if the messengers are not sent out?*
> — Romans 10: 14 (GNT)

In addition, it is crucial to review the relationship between the visionary and members of the team. The visionary could be either

---

[50] *See Habakkuk 2: 2.*

the Pastor or the Pastor's representative in the Worship Unit of the Church. Sometimes, people slack in their commitment as a result of demotivation. If people are belittled, if they feel unappreciated, unloved, feel unwanted; if it appears all you care about is a successful rehearsal or beautiful service, it could affect a person's behavioural output. According to Michael Page, some of the main reasons why an employer can feel demotivated include:

- feeling undervalued
- absence of development opportunities
- poor leadership
- conflicts
- unrealistic workloads.[51]

I quite agree that these are some of the major reasons for demotivation, which invariably leads to a lack of dedication when it relates to people who serve as volunteers. If there is a disparity between the leaders and members of the team, it could sometimes play out in the wrong direction. By this, I mean that, if a leader is too high up there, and inaccessible to his co-workers, it seldom helps, especially at later stages. Besides, what sort of Shepherd tends his flock from a distance? If you are meant to be a Shepherd, it has to reflect in the sort of pastoral care you provide.

---

[51] Michael Page, 'Seven Reasons for Employee Demotivation' (2016): Accessed June 1 2016. http://www.michaelpage.co.uk/employer-centre/development-and-retention-advice/seven-reasons-for-em ployee-demotivation

Undue repetition can also demotivate people. Take another practical scenario where I know rehearsal is to begin at 7pm, and on a standard day, the head of the choir is likely to be late himself or herself, as the case may be. Most people are likely to stroll in from 7.20pm to about 7.40pm, knowing fully well that the leadership is yet to set a good example for others to follow. We may begin with prayers, while we wait for the rest to join us. Everything done is predictable to the core, and sometimes I then have to ask myself, what I truly gained at the end of the day. If the songs rehearsed are demotivating themselves, such systems tend to affect the level of commitment of some members of the group in the future. When these issues are addressed and dealt with, it helps to boost motivation and improve dedication among team members.

On the other hand, if a lack of dedication is linked to other factors such as family issues, the nature of a person's job or business, academics, and the likes; in such cases, the best the leader can do is to understand the situation, and work within those parameters in view. Those who cannot be as committed for genuine reasons should not be guilt tripped or castigated for their inability to do so at a particular season of their lives. At such instances, leaders tend to pray for them with the hope that God blesses their endeavour and provides an opportunity for future availability. For instance, a student may not be able to commit as much during a time of dissertation, or when examinations or course assignments are due. Where this is the case in your ministry, it is hoped that the leader can appreciate the importance of the welfare of members. A worship leader who is pregnant, may and may not be able to commit as usual, and we could go on with other examples why a person's consistency may drop.

Then and again, there is also another factor responsible for the lack of dedication in some. This is known as the *backsliding factor*. At a time when Kings went to battle, David decided that was the appropriate time to take a break. Some 'breaks' are designed to sift the chorister from the place of their blessing. This sort aims to draw the victim away from a place of effectiveness to a state of backsliding and possibly sin. This is another reason why, at the beginning of this chapter, I stated the need for a strong foundation of prayer in the music ministry. A sensitive leader is responsible for knowing the state of God's children committed into their care. *Be diligent to know the state of your flocks, and attend to your herds (Proverbs 27: 23)*. In that place of prayer and communion, God reveals the state of each member of the team and provides the needed wisdom to help prevent backsliding or wisdom to help the fallen to a place of restoration.

By the same token, people management and conflict resolution methods can be a major challenge in the music ministry. These challenges often start off on a small scale and can be quite daunting, distracting and potentially damaging to the productivity of the church in its entirety. Solomon calls them, the little foxes that spoil the vine.[52] These vices can be categorized into three main branches:

---

[52] *See Songs of Solomon 2: 15*

- *the thoughts*
- *the tongue*
- *the actions*

To begin with, there are challenges that begin from the mind. These challenges a choir contends with are sometimes non-verbal, and at other times they are expressed by some who are bold enough to expose their level of thinking. A notable example of this is when some members of the choir are resentful of a particular chorister who excels at solos. When a few persons stand out in their ability to lead worship, or in their delivery of a solo performance, this may arouse envy or jealousy. This could also play out among musicians. For others, it could be a feeling of inadequacy or low self-esteem. They may feel that they are picked on, or that the Pastor or Choirmaster has a favourite, and in some cases, these feelings are assumptions that may be untrue. Even though they occur in the mind, some act out their resentments through indirect channels, like haughty eye contact, moving away from the fellow the resent at a rehearsal, and through other forms of non-verbal communication means.

We then have the challenges that are tongue-related, which generate strife. Chief among these are gossiping, backbiting, exchange of bitter words, derogatory and sarcastic remarks about a person or a subject, et al. Isn't it ironic that, those who are given the divine task of leading others to bless God with the fruit of their lips, are often the most sharp-tongued and sometimes uncensored in our speech and conversations? James describes the tongue as a fire.

> *And the tongue is a fire, a world of iniquity. The tongue is so set among our members that it defiles the whole body, and sets on fire the course of nature; and it is set on fire by hell.* [7] *For every kind of beast and bird, of reptile and creature of the sea, is tamed and has been tamed by mankind.* [8] *But no man can tame the tongue. It is an unruly evil, full of deadly poison.* [9] *With it we bless our God and Father, and with it we curse men, who have been made in the similitude of God.* [10] *Out of the same mouth proceed blessing and cursing. My brethren, these things ought not to be so.* [11] *Does a spring send forth fresh water and bitter from the same opening?* [12] *Can a fig tree, my brethren, bear olives, or a grapevine bear figs? Thus no spring yields both salt water and fresh*
>
> —James 3: 6—12

To succeed in music ministry, a chorister must learn to tame the tongue. This is because, anything short of this, is a contradiction in terms. You cannot use the same tongue designed to lead worship for backbiting, bitter conversations and gossip. Yet one finds so much bickering, excessive talking at rehearsals in some churches. This is one factor that stifles growth, hinders the flow of the Holy Spirit among his people, and creates division in the body of Christ. Some people pay so much attention to what they consider to be the 'bigger' sins, and yet wallow in the sin of slander and talebearing. Great potentials have been frustrated from their places of assignment because of the massive system of meddling in the business of others. You find someone who should be serving God in church, sitting in the pews because of the experiences they may have had when they stepped out to volunteer to serve in the choir or other units of the ministry. In my experience as a worship leader, I watch out for the little foxes and often take a strict approach to ensure, that issues that appear insignificant, do not create an environment where the Holy Spirit will be limited to flow. This sometimes meant that I was misunderstood and perceived to be too strict. However, in reality, the little foxes have a tendency to frustrate the efficiency and productivity of the vineyard in its totality.

The last of the three categories are little foxes which are action-based. Again, in my experience, one seemingly unimportant issue is tardiness—especially to rehearsals. Most Choristers will be early on Sunday morning, as it is customary to be early enough to prepare for the activities of the day. Whereas, some do not give equal importance to the matters behind the scenes. When a musician or singer is late to rehearsals, it produces seven main effects—

- *stifles creativity*
- *frustrates the agenda*
- *minimises ability to meet group target*
- *frustrates the efficiency of those who are punctual*
- *highlights your true position on the things of God*
- *keeps God waiting*
- *stifles personal development and character*

When a person turns up late to a rehearsal, it could stifle creativity in the sense that— if we were meant to sing a song with a descant, and there aren't enough people to do so, the director may be forced to either change the song, take out the descant or limit the creative process. If the soloist who should be leading the song is running late, it may mean, the plans may have to be changed. In the end, one may find that, if the target for the month was a plan to rehearse and perfect eight songs, the group might be short of the original target as a result of what appeared as an innocent incidence of late-coming on the part of some. Late coming is also a form of injustice to those who are punctual. And in some cases, it may be a sign of laxity and complacency. We notice in the story of Esua and Jacob that, one among the reasons why Esau lost his birthright to Jacob was because he arrived late.[53] For what it's worth, Reuben might have saved Joseph from the claws of his brothers, if he had arrived a little earlier.[54] Thomas lost out at the first opportunity to see the resurrected Lord simply because he was a late comer.[55] Lastly, five of ten chosen virgins lost out from making it as a result of late-coming[56]. The price for late-coming can be costly.

Lastly, most worship leaders and musicians agree and can attest to the fact that sound can be a massive challenge. No matter how brilliant your musicians and singers may be, if the challenge of sound is not addressed and taken care of, it could lead to unproductivity and inefficiency in delivery. This is particularly the case in a situation where sound is left at the mercy of untrained engineers. Bad sound can also generate a lot of technical problems and may frustrate the Pastor, the Congregation, the singers, musicians and the sound

---

[53] See *Genesis 27: 25—40*
[54] See *Genesis 37: 29*
[55] See *John 20: 24-26*
[56] See *Matthew 25: 1—13*

engineers themselves. One way to avoid this is by ensuring all staff in the technical, and audio-visual units are thoroughly equipped with the technical and spiritual training required of them to function in the capacity in which God has called them. It has become commonplace to distinguish the relevance of technical training from spiritual training because, some volunteers lack one or the other, and in some instances, the lack both can be said to be the case.

In an ideal situation, the sound should be handled by people who possess relevant training in sound management and who equally possess the fruit of the Holy Spirit. A Spirit-filled sound engineer, is likely to be sensitive to the job, the flow of the Holy Spirit, and sensitive to the direction the Pastor or Worship Team is moving towards. It also requires humility to function at a unit, where one is unseen, yet working extremely hard behind the scenes to ensure quality in audio and visual delivery.

Investing financially into the worship and sound ministry could also help in the overall productivity of the worship outcome. What this means is that, the church should be prepared to cover the cost of training those who are tasked with the responsibility to mananage the sound. In addition, when it is necessary to purchase sound appliances and music equipments, the needed sacrifices should be made. This should not be seen as a burden on the church, but should rather be seen as an investment in the right order. One of David's legacy is the example he shows in investing in the worship ministry. He didn't stop at playing the harp, David was at the top of the game when it came to the acquisition of the latest musical instrument.

> *Another 4,000 will work as gatekeepers, and 4,000 will praise the LORD with the musical instruments I have made.*
>
> −1 Chronicles 23: 5 (NLT)

It should also go without saying that financial investments made to the worship and sound ministries should be well managed and utilised. When resources are spent on the purchase of quality sound appliances and music instruments, those who play and manage these gadgets should give due diligence in looking after them. God also expects that any investment made to our ministries should yield returns at some stage. One good way to produce financial returns is through the sale of audio-visual resources.[57] It is also significant to state that being profitable does not refer to financial returns alone. Even more important is that, this should lead to the expansion of God's kingdom. More souls should be added to the Church by virtue of the investments made in the worship and sound ministries.

---

[57] See Matthew 25: 14-30.

CHAPTER 5
The Pitfalls in Music Ministry

For the world offers only a craving for physical pleasure, a craving for everything we see, and pride in our achievements and possessions. These are not from the Father, but are from this world.
— 1 John 2:16 (NLT)

As attractive as membership of the worship team can be, one major drawback we find is that this ministry, in a sense comes as a package. There are pitfalls to look out for as a musician or worship leader. Regardless of the measure of anointing a Worshipper may possess, there are **three basic** *temptations* (**pitfalls**) that are inevitable during the course of his or her pilgrimage on earth. John describes them in his letter to the early church in Ephesus as, the lust of the flesh [sex], the lust of the eyes [money], and the pride of life [pride].[58] This is somewhat covered extensively in, 'The Price, Plight And Perils of The Anointed' by Gbile Akanni. In the first chapter, the author observes that once a person is genuinely anointed with the power of God, that individual becomes a threat to the prince of darkness.[59] He further asserts that

> He [the Devil] tempts every anointed man in order to blackmail and discredit him. If he ever finds any loophole, he capitalises on it to accuse him and silence him in ministry. He lures him into pits, where he can trap him and finish him. He sets him up at various

---
[58] See *1 John 2: 16*
[59] Gbile Akanni, *The Price, Plight and the Perils of the Anointed*, (Gboko: Peace House Publications, 2002), 10

> times to trick him into sin, especially the sin of pride. The devil often arranges and sponsors agents to entangle a man of anointing, just to puncture his life and his consecration and commitment to the Lord. He uses what a man loves most to entice him into trouble with his God.[60]

A similar sequence is noticed in the temptation of Jesus in Matthew 4: 1—11. Jesus was led by God into the wilderness and was tempted afterwards by the devil. His first temptation had to do with the appetite. He faced a temptation to turn stone into bread. The anointed has the responsibility to guard their calling and ministry against an uncontrolled appetite for food and appetite for sex. Then, Jesus was also tempted with pride. In verses 5—7 of the fourth chapter of Matthew, we see the dart of pride being thrown at Jesus: In my own words the Devil was simply saying; *'If you are the Son of God, then prove it'*.

If you are a chorister or musician, you should be aware of these pitfalls. They confront the singer and musician again and again and again. Situations present themselves in the church, at rehearsals, and at other places, where you are tempted to prove yourself. To succeed, you must become nothing. You must decrease so that Jesus can increase. It is better to take that walk of shame, and allow yourself to be cheated, misunderstood, abused, and undervalued than to prove a point to those who tempt you to do so. Finally, Jesus faced the temptation similar to the lust of the eyes. The devil took him to a high pinnacle

---

[60] *Ibid.*

and promised him the whole world in exchange for worship. What this goes to show is that, even though material success, comfort and acquisitions of goods have their place, a Christian is expected to retain a certain level of contentment and godliness no matter their financial situation.[61]

Occasionally, when things like this are read, one could be tempted to receive the warning for someone else. However, when we look deep down, God may actually be directing the message to us, and not necessarily to those who come to our minds. The temptation of Jesus is a good example of such. Once in a while, we may look at that story with the lens of a scenario specific to Jesus alone. Whereas, in actual fact, every Christian could personalise the counsel here and take necessary precautions to remain unspotted from the corruption that John attaches to the world. On that premise, we focus on the pitfalls that you may call the core day-to-day battles of the anointed musician and anointed worship leader.

While we agree in general that every Christian is a target of the enemy as Gbile Akanni describes; it is also true to assert that the worship ministry is often a prime target of Satan and his cohorts. The chief reason for this is not far-fetched, he occupied a similar position once, as a chief musician and as an archangel. This record is illustrated in Ezekiel 28: 12—16.

---

[61] *See Luke 12: 15, Beware! Don't always be wishing for what you don't have. For real life and real living are not related to how rich we are (TLB)*

"'Son of dust, weep for the king of Tyre. Tell him, 'The Lord God says: You were the perfection of wisdom and beauty. You were in Eden, the garden of God; your clothing was bejewelled with every precious stone—ruby, topaz, diamond, chrysolite, onyx, jasper, sapphire, carbuncle, and emerald—all in beautiful settings of finest gold. They were given to you on the day you were created. I appointed you to be the anointed Guardian Angel. You had access to the holy mountain of God. You walked among the stones of fire.

"'You were perfect in all you did from the day you were created until that time when wrong was found in you. Your great wealth filled you with internal turmoil, and you sinned. Therefore, I cast you out of the mountain of God like a common sinner. I destroyed you, O Guardian Angel, from the midst of the stones of fire.'*

(Living Bible, TLB).

THE PITFALL OF PRIDE

Ezekiel's account of the devil's fall highlights the first pitfall akin to every singer, every musician, every worship leader, and persons associated with the Worship of God: *The pitfall of pride*. To begin, pride emanates from the heart; it is abstract in form. It cannot be touched physically; it can only be discerned or made visible by its after product. Secondly, pride is innate. It is largely human nature. I imagine that there are those who may disagree with the assertion that pride is innate. This might be based on the empirical fact that some people tend to possess elements of superiority complex, while others suffer from elements of inferiority complex. However, regardless of the complexes, pride is associated with the human nature. We can support this inference from two fronts.

1. Matthew 18: 1—4
2. Ezekiel 28: 12—16

In the first scripture, Jesus teaches his disciples on humility by presenting a little child. He then lays emphasis on a process of **conversion** by which humility can be obtained. Three words, stand out here. The first is 'except'. Leaving room for no other option. The second is 'converted' and the third is an infinite word, 'become'. Meaning a process, where a person changes from an original state to a desired or different state. Thus, the process of humility is only acquired by conversion. Nobody is born humble, those who possess traits of humility do so through a decision to be converted in their state of mind and reasoning. Paul seconds this view by stating that in malice, we are to be like children, and as adults in understanding.[62]

From this viewpoint, pride is something that may be locked up in you, and humility is only obtainable through a conscious effort to become a changed person. You know something else? Yesterday's humility is not a warranty for that of tomorrow. Have you ever wondered why some people start off in ministry as very humble and meek people and then end up becoming something else? The reason is that some may think they are humble and may fail to continue to work at it, possibly on a daily basis, and as soon as that becomes the case, they degenerate in the practice of meekness.

---

[62] See *1 Corinthians 14: 20*

In the second scripture, we notice why the devil became puffed up. Ezekiel highlights seven main reasons as to why pride was found in him.

- Intelligence, Wisdom: Knowledge, Academic Attainment, Insight, Oratory, Personae, Intellectual Excellence, and Skill (*Ezekiel 28:4*).
- Wealth: Riches and Power (*Ezekiel 28: 5*).
- Fame, Popularity: Social or Political Acceptance (Model of perfection…*Ezekiel 28: 12*).
- Beauty: Style, Elegance, Grace, Physical Build, [*Sex Appeal, as the world might call it are reasons why a person could become puffed up- Ezekiel 28: 12b*].
- Excellent Style, Fashion: Good Dress Sense, Colour Combination, Jewellery could easily increase one's value over a person with a much lesser possession of the elements in question (*Ezekiel 28: 13*).
- Crafts, Musical Gifts: Talents and Artistry, Excellent Vocal and musical production, **'the workmanship of your timbrels and of pipes was prepared for you on the day you where created'** (*Ezekiel 28: 13b*).[63]
- Anointing: A person's prophetic gifting, charismatic leadership, successful visionary leadership, excellent anointed teaching, ability to heal the sick, raise the dead, ability to

---

[63] *Emphasis' in bold are mine.*

bind and loose, ability to pray like a warrior, and even a person's ordination status could lead to pride *(Ezekiel 28: 14)*.

Here lies the crucial point; pride is multifaceted in form. So, while one individual is proud of his intelligence, another may be boastful about his pedigree in society. Hence, it is possible to be proud in one area and insecure in another. As a result, an inferior complex, in one's physical appearance, for instance, may not deter the individual's pride in academic attainment or in another skill, talent, gifting or grace. Another way to look at it, is in the context of the job of vitamins. For the eyes, it is said that Vitamin-A is crucial, whereas for the skin, Vitamin-D, C and E may be more essential. Where a person suffers from an imbalance in nutrition, it could have unpleasant effects. That is in a situation where an individual lacks sufficiency of a particular vitamin while having enough of another. So is pride! I may be humble in heart about my financial status, and proud over something else I consider myself better or superior to someone else.

This explains why sometimes pride is often left undetected. It can be subtle, and it can be overwhelmingly glaring. Pride can be expressed verbally or non-verbally. You may walk like Mother Theresa, and still be proud. Another individual might walk like a peacock, and we could all conclude in our minds that, by this person's mannerism one can tell he or she is a proud fellow, and that may not particularly be the case. Occasionally, pride can also be underdeveloped. The underdeveloped form is nurtured to exhibit itself in its full-blown nature, at a later time. As this primarily concerns a Worship Leader, let's take an example that paints the picture in its relevant context: A Worship Leader who has never been exposed to invitations outside their church walls, or outside the shores of their country, may become a totally different person when the opportunities begin to unfold. Certain situations shield or hide the true state of a man's heart. A single sister in the choir may become something else when she gets married and becomes settled in life, and we could give many other examples of this kind of pride.

Pride could also be displayed or underplayed. The choir leader may ask you to stand, and in an underplayed form, the person may react inwardly, with something within this line of thought *'who is he to tell me to stand up?'* Demeanour could equally exhibit pride; a haughty eye is an abomination before God. Yet, at the corridors of a music rehearsal, you find a lot of it, among other body languages passed to a group of people or an individual. The bad news is that, whatever form or shape pride comes in, God resists the proud. This is also another reason why some singers and musicians are unable to lead others to God's presence effectively. In some cases, you play the music with skill and excellence, sing the song with all the anointing in the world. Nonetheless, it is safe to assert that, it is difficult to access the holy mountain of God with pride in the heart. The devil's unrestricted access was withdrawn due to pride. I hardly believe anybody else may be spared if a person who was so heavily endowed with beauty, skill, riches, anointing, and intelligence could be disgraced and banished as a result of pride.

The irony of it all is that, while those of us on the earth are components of dust, the devil was made with precious stone. So imagine the scum of the earth full of itself. For this reason, it is advisable to watch out for the pitfall of pride as a singer or musician. It terminates a person's potential and destiny with God. It renders the effort of service ineffective and frustrates God's desire to bless those who labour in his vineyard tirelessly.

THE PITFALL OF LUST

To reiterate what has been stated earlier on, we notice three temptations brought along Jesus' path. *Lust, Materialism* and *Pride*. These three vices remain the same tricks of the enemy today. Any observer of the times can attest to the fact that, great men and women of God have been victims and casualties to a great fall, time and again mainly through one of these windows.

> 'Run from anything that stimulates youthful lusts. Instead, pursue righteous living, faithfulness, love, and peace. Enjoy the companionship of those who call on the Lord with pure hearts.'
> —2 Timothy 2: 22 (NLT)

Anyone who will remain relevant in the unfolding of God's purpose must run from lust. For this reason, it is wisdom to put safe mechanisms in place to protect yourself from pollution. As a worship leader or Christian musician, you are a target for pollution. If the enemy is able to pollute your conscience or body, it automatically goes a long way in affecting the move of God among his people. An example of this truth is seen in the chronicles of Israel. Achan took an accursed thing from the enemy's camp, and because of that, a battle that God had already promised victory to the people of Israel was lost to a very small city called Ai. Joshua could not get a grip of what could have gone wrong. God had promised to go before Israel and had promised to help them conquer the lands and territories. They had already enjoyed victory over a country that was much larger than Ai. Thus, something was definitely wrong. When the children of Israel asked God, what could have led to such a defeat, it was revealed that there was sin in the camp.

The worship must be sanctified. In Psalm 24: 3—4 and Psalm 15: 1-3, God is very clear about the prerequisite for an acceptable form of worship. David in one of his discussions with God wanted to know the requirements for the job of a worship leader, and God gave him a detailed response.

He asked, 'Lord, who may go and find refuge and shelter in your tabernacle up on your holy hill?'[64]

And God categorically replies with the answer—

> 'Anyone who leads a blameless life and is truly sincere.

Anyone who refuses to slander others, does not listen to gossip, never harms his neighbour,

---
[64] GNT

> *speaks out against sin, criticizes those committing it,*
> *commends the faithful followers of the Lord,*
> *keeps a promise even if it ruins him,*
> *does not crush his debtors with high interest rates, and refuses to testify against the innocent despite the bribes offered him—*
> *such a man shall stand firm forever.'*
>
> —Psalm 15: 2-5 (GNT)

Psalm 24: 4 phrases it in one sentence; simply, a person with clean hands and a pure heart. These are very explicit terms for what is acceptable and what is unacceptable. On the converse, what we find is that members of the choir can be very good at selective amnesia. We forget scriptures like this and are quick to recite David's adultery with Bathsheba or how the dispensation of grace provides an exclusionary clause to what is acceptable. Therefore, tacitly or directly implying that grace substitutes God's uncompromising stance on holiness and purity of vessels.

However, one thing we can thank God for is that Romans 12: 1-2, where an acceptable form of worship is re-emphasised happens to be a New Testament scripture and not an Old Testament one. If it were written in the Old Testament, some people might quickly jump at the distinguishing factor between the old and the new. You might also notice that this train of guidance is repeated in 2 Timothy, In 1 Peter, in Corinthians, in Revelations and all over the New Testament. You simply cannot live a life of immorality and function effectively as a leader, musician or member of the choir. Lust in the heart or lust put into practice frustrates the grace of God on the believer and hinders the flow of the Holy Spirit in the gathering of believers. Thus, mechanisms to live a consistent holy life should be put in place, for the worshiper's own good.

THE PITFALL OF MONEY

We then notice a third classic temptation Jesus faces. Again this is repeated in John's letter. As High Priest of our confession, Jesus had to be tempted in every way and was yet without sin. What this tells us, is that we will be likewise tempted to compromise in order to meet our material needs. When the devil offered Jesus the world and its riches, he did so on one condition: **compromise**. Jesus had to make a decision to decline that offer. This brings some relevant concepts to bare. Firstly, this offer was given to the Son of Man who had no place to lay his head. The ability to own a home, or at the least rent a place of your own as a musician or singer is important. That said, its importance must not be achieved on the bed of compromise. Jesus had to go through a limited and restricted lifestyle, as an example to Christians to come (John 13: 15). While he became poor, so we might be rich, these riches are not to be achieved through compromise or any inordinate fashion.

Secondly, Jesus didn't really need the entire world, even though that was what was offered to him. An unnecessary offer was thrown at him, but he was disciplined enough to decline and godly enough to be contented. As a result, God gave him a name above every other name, gave him all power in heaven, on earth and underneath the earth, put all things under his feet, and gave him the keys of life and death. All it took was a momentary period of waiting and a period of long suffering and endurance. As a singer or musician, it is recommended that you also decline the temptations to become materially comfortable on the spot. God may require a timeline of waiting and a time where your character is formed and developed to enable an enduring, sustainable ministry and a victorious end.

> *We can rejoice, too, when we run into problems and trials, for we know that they are good for us—they help us learn to be patient. And patience develops strength of character in us and helps us trust God more each time we use it until finally our hope and faith are strong and steady.*
>
> —Romans 5: 3-4 (TLB)

May I state that, as followers of Christ, we may also find ourselves in between the devil and the deep blue sea. At your worst seasons, the temptation to compromise the integrity and the temptation of what may appear to be a greener pasture is highly probable and perhaps unavoidable. For a young person, this could mean a lot. In Genesis 13: 7—11, Lot found himself in the middle of an awkward conversation with his uncle, Abraham. When he was offered the choice to choose first, he unwisely opted for what appeared greener. Such temptations are thrown at musicians particularly, now and then. You get an offer to play an instrument in a church, and in the midst of what appears uncomfortable, a better offer comes up, and without any careful consideration, some dive into it, and more often than not get hurt in the process.

Now, when paid musicians and singers are confronted with the subject of what is morally right or wrong about the remuneration of services, some among these group become very sensitive and emotional about the subject for various reasons. To set the record straight, the focus here is not on the moral justification for remunerations. It can be argued that a labourer is due his wages, and there are also counter arguments on who rewards and when rewards are due, and what form or package it should come in. What we hope to consider about money, is the principles and integrity required in ministry, and the possible danger, insensitivity to this pitfall can pose. To diffuse any tension, let's agree with the general view that the Levites should be offered their due portion if that is what they are called to do as a vocation. What we focus on here is to bring to your remembrance three basic temptations which provide a framework upon which other temptations rest.

SHOULD A MUSICIAN BE PAID?

This poses the question, how do we draw a balance between musicians who are undervalued, neglected, abused, and overused? One way to answer this question is to decide what school of thought you belong to. There are those who are of the view that our services to God should be voluntary. Those who take this view, consider it from a number of angles. In equal measure, there are those who take a contrary standpoint and believe that a musician is a skilled person who serves God with their gifts, but also does so as a vocation, similar to any full-time minister or preacher. As a person, I take a constructivist view where the answer to these questions, should be based on a person's biblical conviction and understanding. Therefore, sometimes, one has to look at a case by case situation and trust every believer to work according to their conscience, provided that each man can stand before God with a clean slate on the last day. For the sake of those who may be in between both schools of thought and undecided, I shall consider both perspectives briefly and hope that each reader will make up their mind on what they hold to be ideal.

Customarily, a two-sided argument begins with the *pros* and then the *cons*. On that note, I shall start with the support for why some believe that musicians should be paid. In my findings from scripture, I observe biblical grounds for each side of the debate.

> *On that day men were appointed to be in charge of the storerooms for the offerings, the first part of the harvest, and the tithes. They were responsible to collect from the fields outside the towns the portions required by the Law for the priests and Levites. For all the people of Judah took joy in the priests and Levites and their work.* [45] *They performed the service of their God and the service of purification, as commanded by David and his son Solomon, and so did the singers and the gatekeepers.* [46] *The custom of having choir directors to lead the choirs in hymns of praise and thanksgiving to God began long ago in the days of David and Asaph.* [47] *So now, in the days of Zerubbabel and of Nehemiah, all Israel brought a daily supply of food for the singers, the gatekeepers, and the Levites. The Levites, in turn, gave a portion of what they received to the priests, the descendants of Aaron.*
>
> —Nehemiah 12: 44-47 (NLT)

In this scripture, the first thing to point out is that the practice of having choir directors and singers began in the time of David. This practice continued even outside the walls of Israel, at a different era and during Israel's years in Babylonian captivity. While they served God in their places of assignments, Zerubbabel and Nehemiah ensured that they were treated fairly and given their rightful portions. They were not neglected. Furthermore, in 1 Corinthians 9: 7—11, Paul states that a soldier should not go to war at his own expense. Those who labour as full-time servants of God should be evenly catered for.

Sometimes, it can be a bit insensitive to minimise the importance of ensuring the welfare of those who labour in God's vineyard, in this case, the musician. If a musician is expected to be in church for a midweek service, a Sunday service, some rehearsals to ensure unity in what is produced and offered to God in worship, and if excellence and dedication are required for the role they play, in some instances, this may affect their ability to be effective with a regular job outside church walls. There are occasions where some who fall into this category, have no other jobs or sources of income. Where this is the case, no amount of scripture quoting justifies our responsibility to consider the welfare of those committed into our care.

In addition, refusal to be aware of the welfare conditions of those serving in ministry is not a valid excuse, and this is because we are instructed to be careful to know the condition of the flock. The

NKJV instructs that this should be actively pursued with **diligence**.[65] If we fail to recognise that someone who serves at the very front is unable to pay for their transportation to church, how are we able to cater for those who are members of the congregation? Especially as the book of Acts describes a decent welfare system in place in the early church. James 2: 15—17 spells out our responsibility to provide practical solutions to those who are in need.

Hence the welfare system should begin at the front, accommodating those who labour behind the scenes, as in this case, the musicians where it is applicable. It doesn't augur well to organise programmes and invite speakers and guest musicians from other quarters, catering for them with lavish abandon, when the same courtesy is not applied to those who genuinely require attention in our churches. It is somewhat hypocritical to do so. On this premise, a church that is able to afford to ensure their musicians are catered for, should so do.

In the converse, those who make a case against remuneration of musicians do so on biblical grounds in view, and within a context that should be equally understood by anyone who takes a contrary disposition. In my finding, the reason why payments of musicians in a sense are discouraged to find its root in certain principles. Firstly, your anointing and gift should not be monetised for the sake of gain (Matthew 10: 8). What this means is that the primary reason why you play or serve in the church should not be focused on what you

---

[65] *See Proverbs 27: 23. Be diligent to know the state of your flocks, and look well to your herds*

could achieve from it financially. The support giving to remuneration earlier focuses on the relevant need, and genuine welfare of those who serve, it is not focused on people who serve with the motive to get financial rewards from the church. Gehazi is an example of a person who served with filthy lucre in mind, and he paid a huge penalty for his greed and insensitivity in understanding the times.[66]

Secondly, the gift of God should not be for monetisation alone. What do I mean by this? If you choose what church you go to or who becomes your pastor solely on the basis of how much they can pay, that can be a very slippery slope. In Acts 8: 9—24, we are told that as many put their faith and trust in Jesus, Simon the sorcerer claimed to have believed also. Afterwards, he began to follow Philip everywhere he went. Later on, his true intentions were brought to light. He wanted the gift of the Holy Spirit with monetisation of the gift in mind. The reason this point bares importance to this topic is not far-fetched. Sometimes a musician is paid £ABC and then gets an offer of £ZYZ and then takes off from the previous church because of what appears to be a better offer, with no thought of issuing a prior notice to enable the church to find a suitable replacement. While the Scripture makes room for the welfare of God's servants, it is no justification for filthy lucre or greed. Paul reminds us in his letter to Timothy that godliness with contentment is itself great wealth.[67]

---

[66] See 2 Kings 5: 20—27
[67] 1 Timothy 6:6 (NLT)

Thirdly, when the focus is attached to a monetary reward here on earth, it leaves the question of the reward God promises to those who serve him. Do you get paid twice, here on earth and paid for the same thing in Heaven? The Christian race should be carried out with a Heavenly reward in view (1 Corinthians 9:24). Essentially, this means that Christ must remain the focal point in our service to him. He should be viewed as the invisible employer who sees every labour of love and invariably rewards accordingly as the Bible states in Isaiah 45: 19 and in Hebrews 6: 10.

Fourthly, Paul talks about a more excellent way of doing things, and a fellow Levite who shows a more excellent way of dedication to God is Joses. In Acts 4: 36—37, the bible records an account of a man from the tribe of Levi who did things differently.

> *'And Joses, who by the apostles was surnamed Barnabas, (which is, being interpreted, the son of consolation,)* **a Levite**, *and of the country of Cyprus, having land, sold it, and brought the money, and laid it at the apostles' feet.'*[68]

Here we see a Levite who might have been a musician or assigned another task in the temple on a giving day, doing something extraordinary. A person who qualified to receive the due benevolence apportioned to Levites was the one who provided the church with money. Instead of being a Worship Leader seeking to be appreciated for his talent, he made himself the opposite. He became one of the

---

[68] Emphasis in bold are mine.

sponsors of the ministry. For this reason, he was nicknamed a son of encouragement. Whereas some people struggle to pay 10% of their income as God commands, Joses sold his piece of land and brought the entire 100% to the church in order to meet the needs at the time. We are certain he gave everything to the Church because, in the subsequent chapter and verse, we notice Ananias and Sapphira tried to copy him but were not brave enough to give a 100% of the income from their land.

By the same token, David is another good example of a musician who moved from being a receiver to a giver. At the start of his journey, David had to depend on Jonathan to give him clothes. Although He was the warrior who killed Goliath, Saul treated him abominably. He still had to run from pillar to post in search of food. One of the times when he required bread for himself and his men, was prior to his encounter with Abigail (1 Samuel 25: 3—12). Nevertheless, towards the end of his career and ministry, we notice he had moved to a level where he provided more than a million dollars' worth of material for the temple his son, Solomon built for God.

The crucial lesson from these two examples is that, while we can agree that it is okay for musicians to be paid. It is hoped that musicians will model after Joses and David and work towards a level where it becomes more than what you can receive but more about becoming a blessing to God monetarily through giving yourself. This was possible in David's case because his heart was in the right place. From the very meagre amount you receive as a musician or singer, it is important to build a culture of sowing back to God and the work of the ministry as often as God gives you the grace. This is because we also know that where your heart is, there your treasure will also be. We have evidence that David was a man after God's heart, not only through his Psalms but by the very act of his generosity towards God. He never gave what cost nothing.[69]

To conclude, it is better to err on the side of caution than to fall prey to a possible enmity with God. Whatever your convictions may be, do remember that every worshipper will be faced with the temptation of pride, lust and money. Our hope and prayer are that God who prayed for Peter in Luke's account will also be gracious to you, as you take steps to play your part in not yielding to temptation.

---

[69] *See 2 Samuel 24: 24*

CHAPTER 6
The Secret Character of the Worship Leader

> *Finally, my brethren, be strong in the Lord and in the power of His might. Put on the whole armour of God, that you may be able to stand against the wiles of the devil. For we do not wrestle against flesh and blood, but against principalities, against powers, against the rulers of the darkness of this age, against spiritual hosts of wickedness in the heavenly places. Therefore, take up the whole armour of God, that you may be able to withstand in the evil day, and having done all, to stand.*
> —Ephesians 6: 10-13

It was the last Friday of the month. We were either on the verge of entering into the new millennium or we may have just entered it. To ascertain the exact year and time, I would have to peep into my old diaries. For residents of Abuja like myself, and members of 'Redeemed', every first Friday of each calendar month is an appointment at the *Redemption Camp* located at the Lagos-Ibadan Express Way, where over 1 million Christians would gather all night to pray, worship, listen to the Word of God, and most significantly, seek to obtain at least one miracle from God. Then every last Friday, those of us based in Abuja would again gather at the Central Parish for what we called a *State Holy Ghost Service*. On this particular day, right about 5.30pm, I set out of my house for the church because those of us in the choir were expected to converge at 6pm for an event scheduled to commence at 9pm or thereabout.

As was customary for me, I had a culture of eating nothing until after I was certain I had finished all my singing duties in church. Of course, there was a religious undertone or overtone to the culture, being a firm believer of certain principles we observe in the ministry of Jesus and from the parables and stories we are told from the Gospels. As I got to church that evening a little earlier than the allotted time of arrival, I joined other members of the choir; some from different parishes of the RCCG network and others from the same parish as me. We had a choir stall built behind the altar for the purpose of prayers, a brief recap of the songs and arrangement planned for each service, and for distribution of robes and whatever accessories were chosen to accompany our choir uniforms.

It so happens that on this faithful day, as we met at our usual place of convergence, one of the singers graciously decided to hand out some African pastries known as *puff-puff*[70] to everyone who cared to delight themselves in such indulgence. It was unbelievably good value for no money at all since it was a kind gesture. As I watched almost all the other choristers pounce on the *puff-puff*, I resisted the temptation to break my fast before the start of the service, let alone deviate from my personal conviction. Even more so, on a day I was nominated to take a *solo* during a session of the service allotted to the choir.

To make a long story shorter, the time to lead the *solo* finally came, and as I sang my heart out, we had arranged an interval to enable a few minutes of reflection before a loud chorus was to come in. All of a sudden, an unknown individual from the congregation stood up

---

[70] pronounced 'pough-pough' See Glossary for further definition.

and appeared to have a prophetic word for the church. As a result, I listened to what the fellow had to say. After a minute or two, it was obvious this person was either hallucinating or under demonic influence. The Pastors and I take the view that it was rather a case of the latter. I remember very clearly how some of them jumped up on their feet to address the situation, which was nicely dealt with.

In my personal estimation, the crucial lesson of that evening revolves around the feedback we received at the end of the service. We were later told that the manner by which I had comported myself and how God had helped us to handle the situation left no denture or bad taste attached to our song ministration. As a consequence, besides those who really knew what had erupted, most people innocently presumed it was part of the plan for someone to deliver a message in the middle of the song delivery from the congregation. Furthermore, I can only imagine, what it might have been, if I had joined in the puff-puff eating, at a time when my spirit was leading me to fast, pray and remain in a reflective and sober mood. I say this, knowing that Jesus attests to the fact that some demons cannot be cast out except when one has engaged the weapon of fasting and prayer.[71]

As I reminisce over this experience and many other life lessons as a church boy, I realise that my involvement in the choir which has spanned a timeline of 23 years, leave me with an empirical impression of what, to my mind are the core tenets of survival and success in the

---

[71] Mark 9: 17—21

worship ministry. The context and definition of success as it relates to the subject at hand has little bearing with popularity before men. It refers to a place with God, a stake in God's kingdom and a place in the register of the Lamb's book of life. If this counts for anything, I find three core non-negotiables every worship leader must retain through the course of their pilgrimage on earth: (i) Prayer, (ii) The Word, (iii) Righteousness. While I admit, there are tenets of proportional significance such as humility, character, integrity, dedication, and whatever else there may be, I maintain that a life of prayer, the study of the word and a life of holiness serve as the foundation and secret of effectiveness and productivity in the worship ministry.

I'm inclined to believe that a secret place of prayer is the forerunner of a healthy and enduring public ministry. A. W. Tozer covers this in his book, *'Whatever Happened to Worship?'* You'll also find that the *Dake Annotated Reference Bible* observes an important lesson about prayer. Dake found 176 actual worded prayers in the Old Testament, and 46 in the New Testament. Of this 222 prayers made by various individuals, the Psalms records the highest number of prayers made to God in comparison to any other book in the Bible. Of the 72 prayers observed in the Psalms, it is said, that 1 was a prayer of Moses and another a prayer of Ethan; the other 70 are prayers made by David to God. This indicates that even though David, is acclaimed to be a worshipper, we are also certain that David was a person of prayer.[72]

---

[72] *222 Prayers of The Bible*, available at https://hopefaithprayer.com/prayernew/222-prayers-of-the-bible/ Last accessed 12th June 2016.

What is more, we find that the ministry of Jesus was characterised by prayer at the start, prayer as an intricate part of his day-to-day living, prayers towards the end of his ministry and prayers at the climax of his death on the cross. This leaves those who follow in his stead, an example of the role prayer is expected to play in the fabric of our existence. For this reason, a vibrant prayer life is crucial in the worship ministry. Metaphorically, whenever a choir is positioned at the front, instructed to begin the worship service with praise worship, or assigned the task of leading God's people in worship, it is a battle. The only difference the singing plays from the singing in the Old Testament is that in the new testament, the weapons of our warfare are no longer carnal.[73] Whereas in the Old Testament, the children of Israel would go to battle with armed warriors, accompanied by singers and musicians, in the New Testament, we do not wrestle against flesh and blood, but against unseen forces.[74]

This means that, in a counter-attack, members of the choir are likely to be among the first to get hit, if the Shield of Faith, the Sword of the Spirit, the Breastplate of Righteousness and the other weapons of warfare are not put to use. Every move to expand the kingdom of God here on earth is a move against the enemies of God, and in the realm of the spirit, there exists a constant battle. Paul uses this metaphor in his second letter to Timothy —

---

[73] See 2 Corinthians 10: 4
[74] op. cit. 2 Chronicles 20: 21. Also Note Psalm 68: 11-31, Joshua 6:1— 20

> *'Timothy, my dear son, be strong through the grace that God gives you in Christ Jesus.² You have heard me teach things that have been confirmed by many reliable witnesses. Now teach these truths to other trustworthy people who will be able to pass them on to others.³ Endure suffering along with me, as a good soldier of Christ Jesus. ⁴ Soldiers don't get tied up in the affairs of civilian life, for then they cannot please the officer who enlisted them'*
>
> — 2 Timothy 2: 1-3 (NLT)

In a practical sense, it simply means that as a chorister, a life of prayerlessness when engaged in what appears to be a simple exercise of singing or playing an instrument is more than it seems. It is a battle zone. You don't wake up in the morning like a person beside themselves, and just accept to take the microphone to lead praise worship or a song in church, without the necessary spiritual preparations in place. When David was to confront Goliath, he did so with a weapon. He had the choice of going with the physical weapons given to him by Saul, but he opted for something more assuring, he went in the name of the Lord. David made a profound confession to Goliath when he said: *'You come to me with sword, with a spear, and with a javelin. But I come to you in the name of the LORD of hosts, the God of the armies of Israel, whom you have defied.'*[75]

Whenever I get the opportunity to lead the collective prayer with the choir before we proceed to mount the stage consecrated for worship, I would often declare that 'Lord we go in Your name, we go in Your strength and Your power'. The Psalmists puts it in the appropriate

---

[75] 1 Samuel 17: 45

context when it states that, it is not unto us, but unto Your name be the glory.[76] It takes humility to work in someone else's shadows. When you recognise that you may already be an accomplished singer or musician with a certain level of proficiency, expertise and skill, and even more, are aware that God has given you grace and an anointing to sing or play with glee; it takes a lot of humility to still pray before every performance. We have to recognise, remember and retain the position of prayer in our worship lifestyle. They are intricately entrenched together. This is why we pray before we begin a choir rehearsal, and sometimes pray at the end, and pray again before and after our ministry assignments in church.

Now, if you haven't rehearsed the songs to perfection, it makes sense to be nervous, but why, when you know you can easily and comfortably perform it perfectly? If this is how you see it, you have become beside yourself. Those who require God's backing to do what they can naturally do with ease, show it by actions. God can easily decipher where to place you in the scheme of things by your action. The true position of where God stood in the heart of Cain was exposed by the kind of offering he brought to God.[77] You'll also find that, when King Asa was afflicted with a foot disease, to God's amazement, he inadvertently refused to consult God and decided to seek treatment from his doctors.[78] Asa's story is an example of God's perception of prayerlessness. When we neglect him by a life

---

[76] Psalm 115: 1
[77] Genesis 4: 3-5
[78] 2 Chronicles 16: 12

of absolute dependence on skill, and other elements and ways to get what we hope to achieve, it spells out an indirect message to Heaven.

Given these points, how do we develop a lifestyle of prayers in practical terms?

Again, if I were asked, I believe the starting point to a habit of prayer emanates from the activities of the heart and mind. When God confronted Eli, he gave a very nonchalant response to what might have been an invitation for a repentant attitude.[79] This ended his priesthood and also resulted in the termination of a generational heritage in the lineage of Eli. In consequence, Samuel became a ready replacement to Eli. However, when the children of Samuel behaved abominably, in a similar fashion to Hopni and Phinehas, God supported the call for a change of government in Israel.[80] The result was the emergence of King Saul, who in the end also failed to take a humble disposition of repentance when he was confronted by his act of disobedience.[81]

By way of contrast, when David replaces Saul and also falls short, we notice that God took a different disposition.[82] David's kingship was established forever, in spite of his indiscretion with Bathsheba and in spite of the other things he did to tick God off. One major reason why this was the case is linked to four simple facts: David

---

[79] *1 Samuel 3: 18*
[80] *1 Samuel 8: 5—6*
[81] *1 Samuel 15*
[82] *2 Samuel 12: 1—13*

had a contrite heart, a broken spirit, a repentant mindset and a repentant attitude.[83] A lifestyle of prayer begins with a mind and character of insufficiency as an individual and total dependence on God. As a Worship Leader, there are times when I find singing as easy as drinking a cup of water. It comes naturally. However, in spite of the ease attached to the singing, I find that things could go wrong. The musician may forget that their keyboard is on transpose, and play on a very uncomfortable and embarrassing key that messes up the entire arrangement. The backup vocals may find themselves stuck in an unexpected traffic, leaving me to sing on my own, and the possibilities of disappointments are endless. For this reason, over time, we learn to trust God and to rely on his sufficiency.[84]

As a matter of fact, we do not pray only to deter accidents and embarrassing situations. We also pray when we genuinely share in God's burdens. Something in the heart of a chorister should always seek to see the expansion of God's kingdom through them and to see God minister and touch people through healing, therapy, deliverance, repentance, and comfort to the heartbroken, to the hopeless and those in despair. On that account we imbibe a lifestyle of prayer for multiple reasons:

- as a weapon of warfare
- to reflect total dependency on God
- to deter disappointments

---

[83] *Psalm 51: 17*, Also read *Psalm 51: 1—End*.
[84] *2 Corinthians 3: 5*

- to become an extension of God's hands
- to draw revelations from God for every service.

As stated earlier in the first chapter, every service is unique. Every congregation is unique, and every time God's people gather, the needs of the people may differ one from the other. Owing to that fact, the relevant song at yesterday's concert may be irrelevant in today's Bible study. It is only in the place of prayers that we draw inspiration and communication from God to help us to know what he plans to do at each meeting. When prayer is left unsaid, it becomes difficult to flow with God, and particularly flow with the Pastors who are most times people of prayer themselves. Bearing this in mind, a practice of corporate prayers will help the team to sing better from the same hymn sheet. When we pray collectively, at the rehearsals and before each delivery, we are better able to be sensitive to God as a body rather than as individuals. Remember that when Thomas was absent at the first appearing of Jesus to his disciples, he became out of sync with the current move of God at the time. That is one of the objectives corporate prayers achieves.

Above all, we must strive to go beyond the immediate prayers that are made a few minutes before we minister, and also live a life that is true to who we are in Christ. While the aim of this segment is not to condemn any person, it should also be stated that there are practical examples of unhealthy behavioural patterns members of the choir or worship team should deviate from. By way of example, I hardly imagine that a visit to a nightclub on a Friday or Saturday night is a good idea. The contrast of singing and partying all night, and then singing like an angel on a Sunday morning itself is somewhat hypocritical. In 2 Chronicles 5: 11—13, we see that both the Pastors and the Worship Team had to consecrate themselves before the glory of the Lord filled the temple.

This was and still is the standard practice. We need that quiet time away from distractions in order to hear the still small voice as we prepare to minister to God's people. The assignment should never be taken lightly or underestimated. Most significantly, find or develop a lifestyle of prayer that is authentic and personal to you as an individual.

Turning now to the WORD, we can conclusively agree that this is a non-negotiable tenet. In the first place, the foundation of our Christian faith hinges upon the Word of God. It is our manual, our mirror, our map, our constitution, a weapon of warfare, and a device by which God communicates with us. No person can please God without faith, and faith comes by hearing the Word of God.[85] In my own experience, I find that a number of my colleagues survive by the preaching in church. Sometimes, you find people who replace the place of intimate fellowship with God with service in the choir. If I could count the number of excuses as to why singers or musicians like me fail to study the Word on a disciplined and consistent basis, I might be able to purchase something substantially high in price and value.

---

[85] *Hebrews 11: 6, Romans 10: 17*

Whenever I reflect on songs written by Worship Leaders like Don Moen, Chris Tomlin and the likes, I often observe that the lyrics of their songs align directly with verses from the Bible. Their songs provide an insight to a personal walk with God, a reading and study culture that inspires a song in the process. For one thing, the song *Heal me oh Lord, and I will be healed, save me and I will be saved*, is lifted from Jeremiah 17: 14.[86] As you may know, there are many other examples of songs in that calibre which demonstrate a connection between the writers and the influence of their personal Bible studies with their music.

In the second place, God is the Word Himself who became flesh and dwelt among men.[87] For this reason, whenever we study the word of God, we bring Christ to life in our singing and music production. You may be familiar with the popular saying, *garbage in-garbage out*, which suggests that the input determines the output. A singer or musician with no Word has nothing but empty music to offer. It is the Word of God that backs up the demonstration of God's tangible presence in a gathering.

In the third place, God's Word is likened to a mirror in James 1: 23. Who leaves the house without looking in the mirror? How do you lead worship or mount the stage without an idea of what you look like? A mirror is not an object that is used once in a while. It is used as often and as frequent as possible. In like manner, the Bible is not

---

[86] Don Moen, *Heal Me Oh Lord*, (1995: Album- Rivers of Joy)
[87] See *John 1: 1—7*.

designed to be studied or read on Sundays alone. God instructs in Joshua 1: 8, that this book of the law (the Word) should not depart from your mouth, but thou shalt meditate on it day and night, and by so doing, you make your way prosperous and you guarantee success, by God's standard.

In the fourth place, the Bible is the machinery for sanctification. A young man can cleanse his ways by taking heed to God's word.[88] Furthermore, God's word is the only permanent element that can stand the test of time. As a map and guide, every Worship Leader must be entrenched in the reading, and practice of God's Word.[89] As we pay attention to the reading, the study, the meditation and the practice of God's word, we develop into the full stature of Christ. In Peter's words, it is to be desired like milk is desired by babies who would grow. If it is left on the shelf, and hardly ever used, then it creates a problem in the worship team, because spiritual immaturity in such a situation is likely going to stunt the growth of the team, and may also sponsor a lot of strife among members of the team.

Lastly, God's Word is a weapon of warfare. It is the Sword of the Spirit referred to at the beginning of this chapter. It serves as an offensive and defensive weapon in spiritual warfare. While the Shield of Faith and the Helmet of Salvation are defensive tools, a Sword both protects and is equally capable of doing damage to an enemy in battle. God tells us in clear terms to put on the **whole** armour of

---

[88] *Psalm 119: 9, John 17: 17.*
[89] *Matthew 24: 35, Luke 21: 33*

God. To be saved alone and being a jolly good fellow is not all that there is to Christianity. We are to do all to stand, and stand against the evil day. On the subject of the evil day, we can clearly identify the times and a movement of false doctrines afoot, everywhere we turn. Above all, God honours his Word above his name. The Word of God is a surety and guarantee to any and every situation, and for these reasons, we should strive to remain grounded and rooted in the Word.

To summarise, this chapter has pointed out two core nuggets that characterise the foundation of worship that touches God's heart and the elements that play a role in the effective delivery of the trust given to a worship team to edify God's people through music. These are Prayer and the Word. The third element; Righteousness will be discussed in the subsequent and final chapter of this book in the hope that some of the pointers discussed so far will serve as a reminder or perhaps an awakening to the often neglected salient pillars of an enduring worship ministry.

> *'If the spirit of prayer departs, it is a sure indication of a backslidden heart, for while the first love of a Christian continues he is sure to be drawn by the Holy Spirit to wrestle much in prayer.'*
> —Charles G. Finney

CHAPTER 7
Singing and Remaining as One

*For wherever there is jealousy and selfish ambition,
there you will find disorder and evil of every kind.*
— James 3: 16 (NLT)

The moment I arrived Fung's Kitchen, I noticed the double green roofed building with the curve around its edges that seemed to be directed towards the sky; the sort commonly associated with popular oriental architecture. There was also a green roofed pathway directly linked to the building opposite the restaurant. The walls were brownish, and as a novice to building and architecture, I hardly could tell what sort of material the walls were made of. I then inquired from the friend who dropped me off at the restaurant if we were perhaps at the 'China Town' of the city, given that there were a number of Chinese inscriptions all over the other surrounding buildings. The interior of the room was a mix of western and oriental design. As I walked in, I noticed the gold carvings of two dragons fixated on a red painted wall. There were bright lights all over the area, on the ceilings and at strategic places in the restaurant. I was roughly about 15 minutes late. Motoye was already seated at the centre of the room in a table of four. When it appeared I was running later than my estimated time of arrival, she decided to order drinks pending my arrival.

Motoye is a friend I admire so much. She had moved out of London to Dubai and eventually settled down in Houston after her wedding a few years earlier. As we touched base on the usual subjects, we eventually moved to a conversation about the book I was writing. She listened patiently as I shared the main concepts I felt were the key subjects to cover in the project, and when I was done, with a nod of affirmation, she said to me, *'I'm excited about your book, and I pray it will be one of many more to come. One thing, I'll add though'*, she continued, *'is to also highlight some of the factors that help to sustain a worship team'*. Interestingly, I had already written some bits about that aspect but decided to exclude it as part of the subject matter at hand. So, I made my intention to include this chapter known to Motoye, as soon as I got home, and here we are.

As I pondered on my conversation with Motoye two days after, I reminisced on all the opportunities that had come my way, to be part of a choir group in different cities, and at different seasons of my life. I had also hoped that the essence of the subjects discussed in the book would be a reflection of experiences drawn from a multifaceted angle. For example, when I lived in the city of Sheffield, I fellowshipped at a multi-cultural church with people from different nationalities in the staffing of the church. Even though we were not as multiracial as we hoped, we were at the least a people of diverse ethnicities, cultures and nationalities. Our Worship Team was made up of people from South Africa, Zimbabwe, Ghana, Zambia, Nigeria, Germany, Uganda, and the United Kingdom. This meant that we had to learn to function effectively as a team, without losing the essence of our different forms of expression.

For this simple reason, I was able to see how different churches adopted varying *church-cultures* suitable for the vision of each pastor and congregation. At Victory Assembly, Sheffield, I firmly believe we are a strong-knit; jointly tied community, united in purpose. In spite of our unity, we faced similar challenges like other churches. I guess that in my experience, this has been the case in the other Worship Teams I have had the privilege and opportunity to be a part of as well.

On that account, I'm of the opinion that a number of factors help to build and sustain a choir. In the converse, there are equally, elements which deter the spirit of oneness and unity in the Worship Team. To start with, as water is to the human body, so is love to the sustenance of a worship team. If this is absent, everything is likely to fall apart in a matter of time. You will notice that Paul affirms that even the language of tongues without love is like clashing cymbal.[90] God himself is love, and anyone who does not love cannot adequately sing about God.[91] Any such music and singing are a contradiction in terms.

Furthermore, this love ideally should begin from the top. The head of the choir would only succeed at leading and keeping the team together, where he or she is an embodiment of God's love. This love has to be practical and visible. If they cannot feel it, then you have not done your best, or your best is simply not good enough yet. To put this in practice, I shall consider three key principles which align

---

[90] 1 Corinthians 13: 3
[91] 1 John 4: 20

with the style, life and ministry of Jesus Christ of Nazareth, while he was on earth. These are notably:

- *Fellowship*
- *Friendship*
- *Follow-up*

Fellowship

In Mark 2: 16—17, we notice that Jesus ate with his disciples. The message translation contextualises it succinctly:

> 'Later Jesus and his disciples were at home having supper with a collection of disreputable guests. Unlikely as it seems, more than a few of them had become followers. The religion scholars and Pharisees saw him keeping this kind of company and lit into his disciples: "What kind of example is this, acting cosy with the riffraff?"[17] Jesus, overhearing, shot back, "Who needs a doctor: the healthy or the sick? I'm here inviting the sin-sick, not the spiritually-fit.'
>
> (The Message Translation).

Jesus was not too dignified to sit at the same table with his disciples neither was he too high up to eat with them. If we go by general stereotyping, readers from a country with a high *power distance index*[92] will easily attest to the fact that there is usually a disparity between those who lead and those who follow. In a high *power-distance* culture,

---

[92] Geert Hofstede, '*Cultural Dimensions*' (2009): Accessed June 13 2016. https://geert-hofstede.com/national-culture.html

the leader is given a demi-god position where the relationship between the boss and his subordinates is similar to a servant and slave master relationship. Under this culture, a leader should not be seen eating with his followers because this can undermine his authority and the way he or she is perceived. Hence in Churches with African majority, this is not improbable. Eating at a member's house or a wedding is equated to a lack of self-respect in such terrains.

Incidentally, Jesus came from a high power distance index culture. In spite of his cultural background, he took a humble disposition to a lot of things. He is found at the same table with his disciples. At a point, one of them even had the audacity to lean on his chest. Jesus did not enter a separate boat during their missionary trips. If it were today, some people might offer him an exclusive boat, while his disciples tag along in a different one. We are sure of this fact because, on one occasion, while at sea, there was a storm, and Jesus was again humble enough to sleep in the same carriage as his disciples. I like the way Mark put it.

> 'Now when they had left the multitude, they took Him along in the boat as He was. And other little boats were also with Him. And a great windstorm arose, and the waves beat into the boat so that it was already filling. But He was in the stern, asleep on a pillow. And they awoke Him and said to Him, "Teacher, do You not care that we are perishing?'
>
> —Mark 4: 36—38

Thus, Jesus clearly overcame the limitations set by his culture, and he is seen at fellowship with his disciples at all levels. It is not enough to be a leader in the choir practice and church alone. The sort of social life you share with other members of the team goes a long way. Fellowship with others does not demean or devalue your leadership authority, rather it strengthens and validates it. People are able to confide in leaders who are relatable and down to earth. That way you are better able to share in their joy, grief and troubles. You cannot comfort someone over a matter you have never experienced yourself. You cannot claim to be human when those around you have never seen your human side. If all they see is a 'perfect' person who has it all together with a good hair day 24—7, then you are likely to get a half-baked experience of service to humanity.

The dynamics of the worship changes in a group where there is fellowship. People may not be able to explain what it is about the music and the singing, but they can tell that there is harmony. Where this is the case, the congregation is likely to appreciate an abstract impact of power whenever the group ministers. No amount of perfect rehearsals can take the place of fellowship behind the scenes. When brethren **dwell** together in unity, it is good and pleasant.[93]

<u>Friendship</u>

> *'No longer do I call you servants, for a servant does not know what his master is doing; but I have called you friends, for all things that I heard from My Father I have made known to you'*
>
> —John 15: 15

---

[93] Psalm 133: 1—3

In the Gospel according to St John, we find that Jesus calls his disciples friends. This wasn't just a speech; he demonstrated friendship and intimacy on a few occasions. Before completion of his assignment on earth, we notice that beside his pastoral ministry, Jesus also had friends. When Lazarus became ill, a telegram was sent to Jesus intimating him about Lazarus illness.[94] Then in John 11: 11, Jesus makes a profound statement when he tells the other disciples, 'our friend Lazarus is asleep.' This connotes that Jesus was not only friends with his disciples, but also shared mutual friends outside their discipleship circle. They enjoyed extra-curricular activities that had nothing to do with church *per se*. If we find this dynamic in the foundation of our Christian faith, then nothing should stop its existence in the Worship Team. Nothing compares to the harmony you find in a music produced and performed by a group of friends.

Moreover, in a choir where a bond of friendship exists among its members, you'll find that things work better for a number of reasons. Friends bear the burdens of each other, and consequently, when burdens are lessened, people function with peace of mind and tranquillity. Friends also tell each other the truth. A rehearsal is not always a rosy venue. Where there is a bond of friendship, the likelihood of offences, malice and strife are brought to a low. You are likely to take certain things with a pinch of salt if it comes from a friend over someone you consider annoying.

---

[94] John 11: 3. The message was explicit, 'your friend Lazarus is ill'.

In addition, friendship alienates boredom and isolation. When people have no friends in a group, they feel alienated, disenfranchised and disempowered. Under those circumstances, people in that category tend to be silent and unheard. On the contrary, if planted in a friendly environment, those same people tend to share bright ideas and also share laughter.

Life equally abhors a vacuum. *'An idle man'* as they say, *'is the devil's workshop'*. Two will always be better than one, because when one falls, the other is better able to pick the fallen up. If you take a survey, you will find that some people who leave the choir and the Christian faith totally, do so because there was no godly counsel around them. Some were lonely and found friendship outside the walls of the Church. If you go to a club, you will find that there is always someone willing to talk with you, dance with you, and regrettably morally debase themselves. If those of us in church showed a little more kindness and were to offer a hand of fellowship and friendship to others around us, we could make a better impact in our mission to expand God's kingdom on earth.

Follow-Up

The term follow-up is similar to checking up on others. For example, in every choir, you are likely to find those who are witty and lovable. These are the charming ones who are always a delight to be with. They light up a room with their personalities and lessen the rigour of learning a difficult song or the stress of a hard day. Whenever those in this category are absent from rehearsals, it is easily noticed. You also have those who may not be bubbly all the time, yet they bring in a reasonable contribution to the team. Among those in this category are the talented ones who are very skilled in music or skilled in administration and team management.

To highlight an example, when a very good soprano, alto or tenor is absent at rehearsals, it is easily noticed, especially when there are others who rely on them, and some who hide under the strengths of the stronger ones. You then have those who may be new, or who are introverts or easily unnoticed for one reason or the other. Usually, the absence of those in this group is sometimes unnoticed. One quality a good leader demonstrates is to remember that, it is part of their job to notice who is absent and who is present. If any person is absent without the leader's notice, a good shepherd is likely to be dissatisfied with the attendance of the ninety-nine. He or she has the heart for the entire flock and invariably makes an attempt to find out the reason why the one is missing. It doesn't matter if the follow up is done immediately or at a later time. The crucial factor is that follow-up should be done as often as possible. In the instance of Lazarus' illness, Jesus waited for the right time to reach out. It is advisable to religiously follow up those who need it on a frequent basis until they develop and grow to the level where they help to follow up others themselves, thereby making the job of the leader much simpler.

Furthermore, as a leader, it is your responsibility to pay diligent attention to the flock. A good steward gives diligence to the staff

God has left in their care. Part of the Worship Director's job is to be observant. You have to have an eye for every member of the team. The team does better when you understand them when you know what is going on to a fair degree, and when you also seek ways to develop each talent[95]. As a person, I always take a mental or physical roll call at every rehearsal and every meeting. If the drummer or violinist is absent, I would want to know why. It didn't matter what role the absentee played, my first instinct is usually to understand why any person was not at their duty post. You want to know if someone requires prayers or should be referred to the Pastor for counselling because these can also tell if all we care about is the service they render in church, or if we are concerned about their welfare also. These three concepts (fellowship, friendship and follow-up) are foundational components of love expressed. Everything else may fail, but love will always lead to productivity, efficiency and growth of the team.

Turning now to planning, I also realise that success does not come automatically, and this principle applies to the Worship Team. As a choir, you need an annual plan that is clear. In Habakkuk 2: 2 God instructs us to write the vision and make it simple enough for everyone in the team to understand and run with. Even ants plan. They plan for every weather— Spring, Summer, Autumn and Winter.[96] For instance, there are uniforms and colours that are suitable for specific seasons. If these are taken into consideration, it minimises the need

---
[95] See Luke 19: 11—28.
[96] Proverbs 6: 6—11

for squabbles. Besides, if you have a choir with College or University Students, summer holidays and examination periods should be taken into consideration in the annual plan. Everyone should not go on a break at the same time. If the Organist is going to be absent, it ideally shouldn't be the same time as all the altos in the Choir. All tenors should not be absent on the same weekend. An arrangement in order of priority of holidays and breaks can always be agreed by those involved in conjunction with the leadership of the choir and Church Leadership.

What's more, most churches tend to have key annual events usually known in advance. If for nothing else, the Head of the Worship Team should know what the drive for the year is, and should steer their team members in the same direction. For instance, in the RCCG UK, we hold the London Holy Ghost Festival of Life in the Spring and the Autumn of each year, attracting thousands of Christians and non-Christians alike. Those who volunteer to serve in one capacity or another are aware of the annual calendar. Hence besides an emergency, it would be absurd to take a holiday at that time. Attendance and participation to events are usually better when people are accorded the courtesy to plan in advance.

For some teams, plans are also made monthly, and weekly targets and goals are also set in advance. This is not to say that all plans must remain inflexible when drafted. The Holy Spirit may direct a few changes and alterations from time to time for various reasons. However, on the whole, it works much better to be adequately prepared.

When uniforms are also planned in advance, for teams where these are used, it allows room for wardrobe assessments. I shouldn't be told about a uniform arrangement on a Saturday evening, at a time when the shops may be closed. That is a result of poor planning or a gap in communication. Agenda setting at rehearsals can as well be helpful to the Team.

Aside from these major concepts, there are other elements of love necessary in the Worship Ministry. Again, we find that love is patient and kind. It is not boastful or proud. It is not **self-seeking** and keeps no record of wrongs. When such virtues are visible in the choir, it produces freshness and a new anointing at every opportunity for ministry to others through music. Sometimes members of the choir can find themselves in that web of self-seeking and in some cases, it could lead to jealousy or envy. In my team, we would always remind ourselves that it is not about you or me, rather it is about Jesus and his agenda for every gathering. It shouldn't matter who leads the song and who doesn't. Where there is love, the primary attention will exceed the desire to satisfy one's flesh. I have come across people who leave a team because they were never given the task to lead a solo or lead the worship.

I have also come across those who have been envied and disliked for their ability to deliver solos excellently. If you have operated in the music terrain, you'll be all too familiar with the phrase, '*why does it have to be her leading all the time?*' Can't we lead also? Remarks like that tend to lead to strife, and this can be unhealthy for the survival of any worship group. This phenomenon is not new. At a point in Jesus' ministry, we see James and John's agenda at play, when they try to reveal their ambitions of both are becoming the greatest of the disciples. Jesus' response was profound. He did not rebuke them; he simply asked if they were willing to drink of his cup, to which they replied yes. In other words, being ambitious is not the issue, rather the motive is what matters. Ambition for glory-seeking is dangerous, and the antidote to this is the cup of suffering. Greatness and glory come at a price, and the process of payment helps to do away with immature self-seeking and glory seeking in a person's desire to take the spotlight.

In addition, love is not easily offended. A person who is easily offended is like a bad apple in the worship team. Any expectation and hope that those you work with should never upset you or step on your toes is an unfair and impractical expectation. I remember we would preach to ourselves at choir practice, reminding the other person from time to time to make allowance for offense. We learnt to forgive in advance, and this helped to sustain our relationships with each other. Besides, offences are also a pitfall the enemy uses to contaminate an individual's worship experience. As a chorister, it should be obvious to one that offences will be inevitable. The task of sounding like one voice with people from different backgrounds, different temperaments, different experiences and different expectations is by no means an easy one. The process always leads to one misunderstanding or the other, and patience and a heart of love are some of the key virtues which aid a smooth sail from a place of strife to a place of harmony and unity.

Lastly, a system of fairness and impartiality is pivotal to the survival of any worship group. I recall that in one of the choirs I was given the opportunity to lead, we had our share of *divas* and *prima donnas* who had to be put in their place. We had a strict rule about punctuality and absenteeism from choir rehearsals. Any person who failed to attend the rehearsal without good and acceptable notice is not handed a robe or uniform. Simply put, such a fellow was not allowed to minister even if he or she was originally the lead soloist or worship leader. For late-coming, this applied to those who turned up after the final prayers before mounting on the stage is said. However, my prima donna friends occasionally turned up late, and whenever they did, I ensured the rules were followed strictly, and this would upset them, particularly because they happened to be my friends, and would expect that I should understand the factors that may have led to their absence or late-coming.

On some occasions, it appeared as if I was trying to put down some people's gifting or suppress talents. Nevertheless, I chose the difficult part of being misunderstood and stood for impartiality, fairness and justice in our worship team because that is the right thing to do. God is a respecter of no persons. The foundation of a king's throne is built on justice. Once this is missing in any team, it spells potential disintegration. People tend to notice when others are given exclusive and special preferences and privileges over others, and once this cannot be satisfactorily justified it leads to disharmony. God affirms the importance of fairness[97] in through Peter where we are reminded

---

[97] *Also see James 2: 1—7.* We are not to show favouritism towards some. Every person should be treated equally.

that 'God treats everyone on the same basis. Those who fear him and do what is right are acceptable to him, no matter what race they belong to' — Acts 10: 34-35 (GNT)

On this note I close with the song:

Show me how to love in the true meaning of the word.
Teach me how to give expecting nothing in return.
I want to give my life away becoming like you each and everyday.
My Words are not enough, show me how to love.

Open up my eyes that I might really see
More and more and more of You and less of me
By loving the unlovable and touching the untouchable
Let my actions speak louder than my voice

Babbie Mason, *Show Me How to Love*, (1988: Carry On Album)

CHAPTER 8
After All Is Said and Done

*For what will it profit a man if he gains the whole world, and loses his own soul?
Or what will a man give in exchange for his soul?*
—Mark 8: 36-37

I got a text from a friend in the room next door at about 5.30am one morning, asking if I had plans to visit one of the public university libraries in Baltimore later in the day. I must admit, I felt it was a tempting offer, considering I would have loved to find some books or at the least make use of some of the facilities available to visitors like myself. However, for lack of a better word, my meaningless sleep had just been interrupted. By meaningless, I mean, I was up till very late trying to finish the last segment of my manuscript within the scheduled deadline which, by this time had been postponed for the 100th time. Earlier in the day, I had made up my mind that this was the last postponement I would permit. I would complete the book and move on to other projects.

One of the challenges that became apparent as I came closer to the completion of the project was the quandary I appeared to be in. I was no longer sure I wanted a 7th chapter or an epilogue. After many seconds of indecision, I fell asleep. I wouldn't count the nap as adequate or anything special. Perhaps, a good dream could have spiced things up. In its stead, my dreams that night made no sense whatsoever. Owing to that encounter, I really didn't welcome a 5.30am wake up call. As I skimmed through the text further with sleepy eyes, I remembered Ife had suggested we would be leaving the house for the Library at 7.30am. I must have said to myself, 'that's definitely not going to happen'. I wasn't wasted, but I was certainly tired. So, naturally, I went back to sleep hoping to garner an hour or two more of sleep and perhaps dream of something motivating or fantastic.

Ife's text had done its job. I spent the next hour tossing and turning from one side of the bed to the other, but the sleep I had hoped for failed to materialise. Instead, I listened with eyes closed as everybody else got up one after the other to take a shower, get dressed, sing or pray, eat, iron their clothes and whatever else had to be done before they left the house. At 9 am, I finally got up and muttered one of those prayers one would pray to fulfil all righteousness. I jumped out of bed and walked up to the living room which had a dining set on the side, by the kitchen. As I approached the living area in swift succession, Kay was seated right in the chair opposite the room in a sky blue polo shirt and a denim trouser. He was holding a bowl of cereal in his hands, and seemed to be enjoying it. We exchanged the usual pleasantries while I took notice of the lights above him, right in front of the dining area.

He asked again if I was going to be accompanying them to the Library. Without hesitation I told him, *'the spirit indeed is willing, but the flesh is weak'*.[98] I stayed back indoors, alone in the house. After

---

[98] Matthew 26: 41

all, I was near the end of writing, and I had to be certain that I would draw inspiration from God as to how to end the book. For some odd reason, as the end approached, the notes I had previously made seemed not to make much sense anymore. As I saw it, remaining indoors might give me a chance to make the needed changes, and as I followed that line, the final point suddenly occurred to me. The final point was meant to be the starting point!

The starting point for me was my own life. Preach the message to yourself before preaching to the choir! What happens if you write a great book and do all the things you hope to accomplish? What happens in the end, when that day comes when death or rapture comes knocking? All of a sudden I watch as my soul departs from my earthly body, and then I find myself being transported supernaturally into the sky, one cloud to another, and finally, I arrive at the border control, where all souls must assemble to ascertain their final destination. I then reflect on all my mistakes, my second chances, lost opportunities, my passion for Christ, my love for the things of God, my many struggles and attempts to wiggle my way out of the direction of the Spirit and all the times I let the flesh win. As I think on the good, bad and ugly, I quickly mutter a word of prayer asking God to help me.

For some of us who have experienced salvation and have walked in the grace and calling of God, and tasted a part of the riches of Christ's glorious inheritance, we know fully well, that the worst thing that could ever happen to any person is to be a 'SIGNPOST'. Paul contextualises it by his words in 1 Corinthians 9: 27:

I discipline my body like an athlete, training it to do what it should. Otherwise, I fear that after preaching to others I myself might be disqualified (NLT).

A SIGNPOST points a traveller to the right direction. However, a sign post remains on the same spot. It is never found in the destination itself. Regrettably, any person who sings in the choir, plays an instrument in church, serves God, and yet fails to discipline the flesh and live a life that is holy and pleasing to God is only hinting at one possibility. That is, 'my singing, church going, clapping and all this is a waste of time'. I am hopeful that this will not be your testimony nor mine. We are not designed to show others the way to salvation alone. We were designed to be first reconciled with God. You are only giving a ministry of reconciliation, with a task of uniting nonbelievers with Christ, when you have been reconciled to God yourself.[99]

In most cases, members of the choir have to spend money on uniforms and transportation to an uncountable number of rehearsals and church events. We spend time setting up the instrument before the service, packing up the instrument after the service. We attend preliminary meetings designed to plan ahead of certain events and spend hours rehearsing our skills, either collectively or individually. We tolerate and accommodate all sorts of shenanigans for the sake of the Gospel. We sometimes have to submit our personal preferences to accommodate a decision that is made as part of being a team. In

---
[99] See *2 Corinthians 5: 17—18*

the process of service, we are also bruised by the wounds of fellow believers, we are constant targets of the enemy's attacks, and often ride on the wings of God's grace and mercy. I imagine that there should be promising rewards for these efforts and I do not believe that such efforts should be in vain.

A Christian who knows the concept of the Christian doctrine knows that there is life after death. A fellowship in Heaven, a Choir of Angels, Cherubim and Seraphim. The Christian also knows that there are twenty and four elders who cast their crowns before God, crying *'Holy, Holy, Holy is the Lord God Almighty'*.[100] I hardly believe any Christian Singer or Musician can feign ignorance of Christ's death, Christ's burial, Christ's Resurrection, Christ Return, and Christ's Promise to every believer. The totality of our Christian faith rests upon the core doctrines of Christ. He came to the earth with a clear mission– To seek and to save the lost. When the birth of Jesus was foretold, Christ's mission statement was made clear:

> *'And she will have a son, and you are to name him Jesus, for he will save his people from their sins'.*
>
> —Matthew 1: 21 (NLT).

This brings us back to the third secret nugget of successful ministry from the lens of a Heavenly citizen. This is either referred to as righteousness or holiness. It is the principal prerequisite for admittance into God's kingdom. Solomon contextualises this in a simple fashion

---

[100] Revelations 4: 8, NLT

when he tells us that in the end, we have only two duties, that is (i) to fear God and (ii) to keep his commandments.[101] You may agree that Grammy Awards and all other forms of earthly recognition, alone do not cut the deal, and the reason for this is paraphrased in two of the most crucial rhetorical questions ever asked in the history of the world:

> *For what will it profit a man if he gains the whole world, and loses his own soul? Or what will a man give in exchange for his soul?*
> — Mark 8: 36—37

From the preceding text, as we pursue our various goals and dreams, we must retain a righteous standing with God because when we study the bible, we find that God keeps records of our stewardship. You do not just sing as part of a worship team. There is a record with your name in it, and with a record of your punctuality, attendance, faithfulness in the secret and in the open. There is a record of your daily conversations and conduct with the saved and unsaved, a record with the hidden thoughts of the heart, and a book with a record of those who remain unspotted from the corruption in the world. It also doesn't matter if you are a millennial, baby boomer, young or old. Each and every one of us shall stand to give an account of our lives to God.

> *I saw the dead, both great and small, standing before God's throne. And the books were opened, including the Book of Life. And the*

---

[101] *Ecclesiastes 12: 13*

> *dead were judged according to what they had done, as recorded in the books*
>
> —Revelations 20: 12 (NLT)

As we draw to a close, the issue of the signpost brings to mind a remark Jesus made to some of the virgins who were espoused to be married to him. *But he answered and said, Verily I say unto you, I know you not*[102]. This statement was made to 5 of 10 virgins. It was a remark to a group of people who were already close to the finish line. This goes to show that the closer you are, the more careful you must be. Never get to the place where the regularity of the singing and service in church becomes a deterrent to a healthy relationship with God. We must also remember that Moses' conversation with God proves that a name could be removed from the book of life (Exodus 32: 32).[103] David confirms this in Psalm 69: 28 and Jesus provides the master stroke in Revelations 3: 5 where he gives a condition upon which a person's name is retained in the book of life. From Christ's very words it has been said that:

> *He who overcomes shall be clothed in white garments, and I will not blot out his name from the Book of Life; but I will confess his name before My Father and before His angels.*
>
> —Revelations 3: 5

If this is the case, I charge you to ask yourself either of two questions.

---

[102] *Matthew 25: 12*
[103] Enoch A. Adeboye, '*The Book of Life*': *The Power, Praise & Purity Bible* (Cambridge: Cambridge University Press, 2003), 82.

- o   Is my name written in the book of life? or
- o   Is there any chance my name has been blotted out of the book?

The certainty of what the answers to these questions are will only be ascertained on that day when the trumpet shall sound, or on the day when God calls a person home. However, in the interim, if in your heart you find an uncertainty and fear lingering, it can be an indicator, that you may need to make your ways right with God, either by renouncing any unconfessed sin that is displeasing to God, or by a renewal of your commitment to God. (For those who are already in a c committed relationship with Christ). As for those who wish to do so right away, do remember that God is omnipresent. This means that he is present everywhere including wherever you are as you currently read these words. So, find a prayer below that can be used as a starting point, or feel free to make your own prayer that reconnects you to God.

> *Dear Lord Jesus,*
> *I acknowledge that I have sinned and fallen short of your glory.*
> *Please forgive me.*
> *From today, I make a commitment to be reconciled with you,*
> *Knowing that those who come to you are never rejected.*
> *I confess that Jesus is Lord and Saviour, and I recognise that you are able to save to the uttermost.*
> *I renounce every sin and every habit that has separated me from you, and I accept your forgiveness.*
> *Write my name in the book of life and from this day, give me the grace to live for you.*
> *Thank you for hearing and answering me, in Jesus' name. Amen!*

If you said that prayer, I congratulate you because all it takes is a believing heart and a mouth which produces salvation. *For with the heart, one believes unto righteousness, and with the mouth confession is made unto salvation.*[104] Now, what you do next matters. From God's perspective, after you have been forgiven, saved and restored, you are expected to live differently. If you require further counselling, kindly find a bible-believing church near you or feel free to contact me via social media.

@SILASWORSHIP

---

[104] *Romans 10: 10*

GLOSSARY

Ad lib — *a music terminology derived from the Latin phrase, ad libitum. An improvised addition in a song. This is usually led by the soloist or lead singer.*

American Idol — *An American singing competition Television Series.*

Backsliding Factor — *A relapse into error or into a person's former ways*

Compendium — *A collection of detailed information*

Cons — *Short for the Latin word— Contra. Also see pro*

Cultural Dimensions — *The degree to which the less powerful members of a society accept and expect that power is distributed unequally.*

Diva — *See Prima Donna. The original definition is a female singer in an opera. In contemporary terms, this refers to someone who thinks he or she is better than everyone else and who does not work well as part of a team or group.*

Incommunicado– *To be out of reach. Not wanting or not able to communicate with other people.*

I-tunes — *A media library and media play developed by Mac Incorporation.*

Kyrie — *(Latin) A prayer for mercy often sang or spoken in a Catholic Church Mass*

Liturgy — *A formulary for the celebration of Christian worship, particularly in the Catholic Church.*

Mass — *Sacrament of the Eucharist.*

Middle-Belt — *Central parts of Nigeria that are neither North nor South within a geographical framework*

Nicene Creed —*A profession of faith commonly used in a liturgy*

Penitential Act — *Confessions made at the start of every Mass*

Power Distance Index (Dimension) — *This dimension expresses the degree to which the less powerful members of a society accept and expect that power is distributed unequally. The fundamental issue here is how a society handles inequalities among people. People in societies exhibiting a large degree of Power Distance accept a hierarchical order in which everybody has a place and which needs no further justification. In societies with low Power Distance, people strive to equalise the distribution of power and demand justification for inequalities of power.*

Prima Donna — *Original definition is a chief singer in an opera or opera company. In contemporary terms, this refers to someone who thinks he or she is better than everyone else and who does not work well as part of a team or group.*

Pro — *in the singular form. Usually 'Pros' in the plural form. Pro and Cons derives its origin from Latin meaning; 'for and against', 'pro and contra'. Synonym: Advantages and disadvantages.*

Providence — *A divine intervention or direction*

Puff-puff — *French:* **Beignet**. *A West African pastry made from flour, sugar, yeast, water and oil.*

RCCG — *An Abbreviation for the Redeemed Christian Church of God.*

Redeemed — *A Nigerian colloquial term for members of the Redeemed Christian Church of God.*

Redemption Camp — *RCCG Head-Quarters located around the Lagos-Ibadan Express way in Nigeria.*

Sister Act — *A 1992 American comedy film where Whoopi Goldberg stars as an undercover nun.*

Sol-Fa-Notation — *Also known as Tonic Sol-fa. A technique used for reading music, by which sol-fa syllables do, re mi, fa soh are used.*

Solo – *A piece of vocal or instrumental music for one individual. It can also be a part of the music allocated to one singer or player.*

Spotify — *A software device linked to the internet which provides an exhaustive library of music from all over the world.*

Stereotyping — *The general norm and standard practice in a society. Stereotypes often miss out on the possible exceptions to the norm.*

Tête-à-tête – *A private conversation between two people.*

Thump Thump- *A figure of speech known as onomatopoeia which relates to the description of a thing with the use of sounds.*

Transpose — *Also known as transposition. It means playing or writing music in a different key.*

YouTube — *A website that provides an extensive number of videos from all over the world.*

X-Factor — *A British reality television show that encourages auditions, showcasing of talents, and a music competition.*

BIBLIOGRAPHY

Adeboye, Enoch. *'The Book of Life', The Power, Praise and Purity Bible*, Cambridge: Cambridge University Press, 2003.

———. *The Role of the Choir, Lecture delivered at the Redeemed Christian Church of God UK Annual General Meeting London*, November 18, 2004.

Akanni, Gbile. *The Price, Plight and The Perils of the Anointed*, Gboko: Peace House Publications, 2002.

Brown, Brenton and Riley, Ken, *Everlasting God*, Brenton Brown, Integrity Music, 2006, CD.

Caesar, Shirley, *A Miracle in Harlem*, Word Entertainment LLC, 1997, CD.

Cho, David Yonggi, *The Holy Spirit, My Senior Partner*, Mary Lake FL: Charisma Media, 1989.

Ellis, Christopher, *Approaching God: A Guide for Worship Leaders and Worshipers*, Canterbury: Canterbury Press, 2009.

Finney, Charles, *Charles G. Finney: An Autobiography*, Chicago: Fleming H Revell Company, 1908.

Graham, Billy, *NKJV, The Billy Graham Study Training Centre Bible*, Nashville: Thomas Nelson, 2006.

Hagin, Kenneth E., *Understanding The Anointing*, Tulsa: Faith Library Publications, 1983.

Hofstede, Geert, *Cultural Dimensions*, available at Geert Hofstede Website: https://geert-hofstede.com/national-culture.html

Ishmael, Odeen, *Reciprocity in International Relations*, 2013.

Kenoly, Ron, *The Effective Praise and Worship Leader*, Stafford: Parsons Publishing, 2008.

Mason, Babbie, *Show Me How to Love*, Carry On Album, 1988.

Moen, Don, *Heal Me Oh Lord*, Album- Rivers of Joy, 1995

Munroe, Myles, *Understanding The Purpose and Power of a Woman*, New Kensington: Whitaker House, 2001.

Page, Michael, 'Seven Reasons For Employee Demotivation', http://www.michaelpage.co.uk/employer-centre/development-and-retention-advice/seven-reasons-for-em ployee-demotivation, accessed on 12th June 2016.

Peterson, Eugene H., *The Message Bible*, Nashville: NavPress, 2014.

Smith, Martin., *I Could Sing of Your Love Forever*, © 1995, Delirious?, Sparrow Records, 2001, CD.

Soanes, Catherine and Hawker, Sarah (ed), *Oxford English Dictionary for Students*, Oxford: Oxford University Press, 2006.

222 Prayers of The Bible, available at https://hopefaithprayer.com/prayernew/222-prayers-of-the-bible/ accessed 12th June 2016.

Rickkers, Doris and Tayor, Jeannette, *NLT The Way Finding Bible* (2013: Tyndale House)

Tyndale House, *The Living Bible*, TLB (1974: Tyndale House)

American Bible Society, *The Good News Bible* (2008: American Bible Society)

ABOUT THE AUTHOR

Silas was born and raised in Nigeria; he attended the University of Jos for two years before moving over to the United Kingdom to study for his A level and undergraduate and postgraduate degrees. During that time, he immersed himself in serving Christ as a worker, worship leader, and worship director with his local church. His tireless and relentless service in the "small" paved the way for his contribution as worship leader with the Redeemed Christian Church of God (RCCG), UK central office—a nonprofit based church organization with branches in more than 120 nations of the world. His unwavering dedication to Christ, expressed in his worship has opened doors to ministry across nations and continents.

As a worship director in the RCCG UK, Silas is an astute voice instructor, music director, and worship leader who brings a meticulous and detailed dimension to the teaching, learning, and delivery of songs. His penchant for corporate prayers and corporate worship is a visible trait often admired by many. Silas also serves as vice president of the Pastors' and Ministers' Seed Family UK—a fellowship for children of pastors and ministers.

His first published book, 'The Last Time You Sang to Me', throws light to a compendium of his rich and practical experience in the worship ministry.

Silas holds a bachelor of arts degree in international relations and English and a master of arts degree in global affairs and diplomacy from the University of Buckingham and finds his niche working as a training consultant and music instructor for start-up choirs and worship teams in the RCCG.

Printed in Great Britain
by Amazon